How to Be a Brilliant SENCO

Helen Curran's invaluable book aims to support new and experienced SENCOs with the task of developing and leading special educational needs provision and inclusive practice, through the exploration of practical strategies and approaches.

This book takes a pragmatic approach to the issues which have historically been associated with the role of the SENCO; namely a lack of time, a lack of resources and often a lack of seniority. The book seeks to provide SENCOs with tried and tested ideas and strategies to support both the operational and strategic aspects of the role, to help SENCOs develop their role as a leader in school. The book covers the following areas:

- The SENCO role in policy and practice
- The SENCO as a leader
- Developing relationships with pupils and parents
- Challenges and opportunities within the role of SENCO

A must read for any SENCO, this book draws upon case studies and real life examples, considering the ways in which SENCOs can shape and develop the status of not only their role, but also SEN and inclusive provision in their setting.

Helen Curran is a senior lecturer in SEN at Bath Spa University. She trained as a primary school teacher, later becoming a SENCO, assistant head teacher, local authority advisor and dyslexia consultant. Helen's research focuses on SEN policy and the SENCO role; she is passionate about advocating for SENCOs, and the positive impact they can have on children, young people and families.

Helping Everyone Achieve ■ ■ ■

nasen is a professional membership association that supports all those who work with or care for children and young people with special and additional educational needs. Members include teachers, teaching assistants, support workers, other educationalists, students and parents.

nasen supports its members through policy documents, journals, its magazine *Special*, publications, professional development courses, regional networks and newsletters. Its website contains more current information such as responses to government consultations. **nasen's** published documents are held in very high regard both in the UK and internationally.

For a full list of titles see: https://www.routledge.com/nasen-spotlight/book-series/FULNASEN

Other titles published in association with the National Association for Special Educational Needs (nasen):

How to Be a Brilliant SENCO: Practical Strategies for Developing and Leading Inclusive Provision
Helen Curran
2019/pb: 978-1-138-48966-0

Successfully Teaching and Managing Children with ADHD: A Resource for SENCOs and Teachers, 2ed
Fintan O'Regan
2018/pb: 978-0-367-11010-9

Brain Development and School: Practical Classroom Strategies to Help Pupils Develop Executive Function
Pat Guy
2019/pb: 978-1-138-49491-6

Essential Tips for the Inclusive Secondary Classroom
Pippa Whittaker and Rachael Hayes
2018/pb: 978-1-138-06501-7

Time to Talk: Implementing Outstanding Practice in Speech, Language and Communication, 2ed
Jean Gross
2018/pb: 978-1-138-28054-0

The Post-16 SENCO Handbook: An Essential Guide to Policy and Practice
Elizabeth Ramshaw
2017/pb: 978-1-138-65465-5

Supporting Children with Behaviour Issues in the Classroom, 2ed
Sarah Carr, Susan Coulter, Elizabeth Morling and Hannah Smith
2017/pb: 978-1-138-67385-4

Supporting Children with Cerebral Palsy, 2ed
Rob Grayson, Jillian Wing, Hannah Tusiine, Graeme Oxtoby and Elizabeth Morling
2017/pb: 978-1-138-18742-9

How to Be a Brilliant SENCO

Practical Strategies for Developing and Leading Inclusive Provision

Helen Curran

 Routledge
Taylor & Francis Group

LONDON AND NEW YORK

First published 2020
by Routledge
2 Park Square, Milton Park, Abingdon, Oxon OX14 4RN

and by Routledge
52 Vanderbilt Avenue, New York, NY 10017

Routledge is an imprint of the Taylor & Francis Group, an informa business

British Library Cataloguing-in-Publication Data
A catalogue record for this book is available from the British Library

Library of Congress Cataloging-in-Publication Data
A catalog record has been requested for this book

ISBN: 978-1-138-48965-3 (hbk)
ISBN: 978-1-138-48966-0 (pbk)
ISBN: 978-1-351-03722-8 (ebk)

Typeset in Sabon
by Swales & Willis, Exeter, Devon, UK

To Phoebe, Jamie and Neil
With love

Contents

Acknowledgements x

1 Introduction 1

Aims of the book 3
Organisation of the book 3
A note of caution 4

2 The SENCO role in policy and practice: beginnings to present day 6

The beginnings of the SENCO role 7
The SENCO role today: responsibilities as determined by
   the 2015 SEND Code of Practice 12
The SENCO role in practice 14
Shaping your SENCO role 17
In summary 19

3 The SENCO as a leader: your role, your school, your ethos 22

The SENCO as a leader: should I be operational, strategic or both? 23
Leading on what? Developing and understanding your ethos towards
   inclusion 27
Leading on what? Developing your understanding of the
   definition of SEN 34
Setting longer-term, strategic priorities 37
In summary 38

4 The SENCO as a leader: to be or not to be on the senior leadership team 41

The role of the SENCO and the senior leadership team (SLT) 42
I'm not on SLT, but I think I should be 45
The status of the SENCO role 46

Leading without being part of SLT: leading with status 49
Developing your status as a brand new SENCO 49
Developing your status as a more established SENCO 51
Creating priority through a development plan 54
In summary 55

 Leading and supporting colleagues   58

Introduction 58
The SENCO role: leading and supporting colleagues 59
Unpicking the role of teachers 61
Leading and supporting colleagues: a whole-school approach 63
Leading and supporting specific groups 74
In summary 76

 Developing relationships: pupils and parents   78

Introduction 78
Children and families at the centre: the policy context 80
Pupil relationships: why these are important 82
Family relationships: why these are important 83
Are you meeting the SEND Code of Practice guidance? 84
An awareness of potential barriers 84
Pupil relationships: whole-school approaches 88
Pupil relationships: individual approaches 89
Family relationships: whole-school approaches 90
Family relationships: individual approaches 95
Specific circumstances: Education, Health and Care plans 98
It's not always going to go how you planned 98
In summary 99

 Managing your role: challenges and opportunities   101

Time and workload 102
Resources 109
It's not just you: grow your networks 111
Managing the National Award for SEN Coordination 114
In summary 118
*Appendix 7.1: guidance for SENCO time allocation by school
   size and cohort 118*

8 The future SENCO role   126

*Wider educational changes and how these may impact on
   the future SENCO role 126*
Shaping your future SENCO role 130
In summary 131

Appendix: acronyms   133
Index   134

Acknowledgements

Thank you to all the SENCOs I have worked with over the years, through my research and through the National Award for SEN Coordination. You are all superheroes!

Special thanks to Ally, Chris, Edward, Gemma, Jonathan and Lizzie who took the time to read and share with me their feedback on the ideas within this book.

1 | Introduction

The introduction of the Special Educational Needs and Disabilities (SEND) reforms in 2014 were hailed, by the then coalition government, as 'the biggest transformation to SEND support [in schools] for thirty years' (DfE, 2014a). Whilst the seeds of such change can be traced back in educational policy, the 2006 House of Commons Education and Skills Committee report, *Special Educational Needs* (House of Commons Education and Skills Committee, 2006), was fundamental in highlighting the failings of the then current SEN system. Whilst the report did not suggest a major review of the system was needed, or indeed planned, the report did conclude that SEN needed to have greater priority within education. Other aspects, such as greater clarity regarding the term inclusion and an increased focus on the role of children and parents, were also stated as a necessary improvement. A series of recommendations were made in light of the findings.

The concerns outlined with the House of Commons Select Committee report (2006) were later echoed in the Lamb Inquiry (DCFS, 2009), which investigated parental confidence in the SEN system. *The Special Educational Needs and Disability Review: A Statement is Not Enough* further added to this developing narrative stating, 'the review found widespread weaknesses in the quality of what was provided for children with special educational needs and evidence that the way the system is currently designed contributes to these problems' (Ofsted, 2010, p. 7). This led to the publication of the Green Paper, *Support and Aspiration: A New Approach to SEND* (DfE, 2012). The Green Paper set out the coalition government's vision for the new SEND system and was focused on delivering a system which identified needs early and focused on outcomes for children and young people with a long-term, aspirational view. Central to the SEND reforms was the idea of authentic parental participation, with a specific focus on engaging the views of the child and the child's parents and carers.

The culmination of this process resulted in the 2014 Children and Families Act. Statutory guidance setting out the legal framework for the execution of this act followed and was published in July 2014; *The Special Education Needs and Disability (SEND) Code of Practice: 0 to 25 years* (DfE and DoH, 2014). Small amendments followed with the current version of the SEND Code of Practice published in January 2015 (DfE and DoH, 2015). The requirements of the statutory guidance were due to be implemented in the early years providers, schools and colleges from 1st September 2014. The term *SEND reforms* has been adopted as an all-encompassing term to refer to the legal and statutory guidance presented to schools.

The central principles of the SEND Code of Practice (DfE and DoH, 2015) state that the system should be outcome focused and aspirational, with children and families at the centre. The guidance aims to create a system which is less confrontational and adversarial, and contains some key changes from the previous 2001 Code (DfES, 2001). These include the extension of focus from 0–25 years, greater collaboration between education, health and care and the replacement of School Action and School Action Plus categories of SEN with a single SEN Support category. Previous statements of SEN were replaced with the more holistic Education, Health and Care (EHC) plan. Schools were required to contribute to the local authority (LA) Local Offer, a central repository for transparent and accessible information for parents, and also had to produce a school SEN information report which detailed processes and provision for children with SEN in school, and which is updated annually.

However, despite these changes to the new SEND Code of Practice (DfE and DoH, 2015), the role of the Special Educational Needs Coordinator (SENCO) remained consistent and central within the guidance. The role is still statutory, and it is still a requirement for SENCOs to gain the National Award for SEN Coordination (NA SENCO) within three years. Expectations regarding both the operational and strategic elements remain and the guidance provides, as per previous Codes (DfE, 1994; DfES, 2001), an overview of the potential responsibilities of the SENCO, all of which relate to the inclusion of children with SEN within mainstream schools. It could also be argued that the introduction of the new SEND Code of Practice highlighted not only the importance of the SENCO role, but also its strategic nature, as SENCOs were required to facilitate the changes related to the new guidance in their settings.

Such prominence of the role in education makes this book not only timely, but also relevant. The SEND Code of Practice (DfE and DoH, 2015) is based on inclusive principles, with provision for vulnerable learners, including those with SEN, a priority for all teachers; this is a principle echoed by the national curriculum (DfE, 2014b). It is also underpinned by principles related to the importance of parent and child choice, participation and decision making. These are arguably principles which require whole-school recognition and development to be fully implemented. Therefore, this further highlights the importance and responsibility of the SENCO role.

Aims of the book

The book seeks to provide practical 'how to' guidance which provides predominantly new, but also experienced, SENCOs with tried and tested tips, strategies and case studies to enable them to 'get the job done', from both an operational and a strategic perspective. The mission of the book is to support SENCOs in developing ways of working which enable them to move beyond 'firefighting' and support them to enact the role in a considered, strategic manner. The book considers the issue of whether the SENCO is part of the senior leadership team (SLT), but acknowledges that this is different in many settings, and therefore seeks to present ways in which status can be developed to enable the SENCO to effect change regardless of the seniority of their position within the school. This book aims to consider, and pragmatically accept, the known barriers to the role, including a lack of time, but equally seeks to present an alternative way of executing the role within these known barriers so SENCOs can not only 'get the job done', but do so in a strategically effective manner.

I have spent most of my professional life working with SENCOs in one guise or another. The book is based on my experiences as a SENCO, a local authority SEN Advisor, SEN Consultant and, latterly, a lecturer on the NA SENCO. Through my work on the NA SENCO I have had the privilege to work with over 350 SENCOs. During our sessions we have explored issues related to the facilitation of the SENCO role, we have discussed and debated tried and tested strategies and tips, as well as developed our own. The book is also based on my research which has explored how SENCOs effectively implement policy in their settings and how they manage their workload. For me, this is the most important role in school, because good inclusive practice is good practice for all.

Organisation of the book

The book is organised into the following chapters:

- The SENCO role in policy and practice: beginnings to present day.
- The SENCO as a leader: your role, your school, your ethos.
- The SENCO as a leader: to be or not to be on SLT.
- Leading and supporting colleagues.
- Developing relationships: pupils and parents.
- Managing your role: challenges and opportunities.
- The future SENCO role.

Within each chapter you will find:

- Ideas in action: examples, case studies and/or practical advice on how to enact specific strategies or how to approach particular problems.
- Something to think about: questions, comments and moments of reflection to encourage you to think about your own setting and consider the actions or changes you could make to improve practice.

A note of caution

The book is intended to be used as a toolbox. The book is intentionally filled with actions and strategies, processes and changes you can introduce to effectively facilitate the role of the SENCO in your school and, as a consequence, improve inclusive practice and outcomes for children and young people with SEN. However, this is not intended as a 'tick list'. Read the chapter which is most relevant to you currently. Consider the ideas and pick two or three which you can try out – save the rest for later. The idea is to view the development of SEN and inclusive practice in the longer term.

Note: the following terms are used interchangeably throughout the book:

- Child/children/young person/pupil.
- Parent/carer/families.

References

Children and Families Act 2014, ch. 6. Available at: www.legislation.gov.uk/ukpga/2014/6/pdfs/ukpga_20140006_en.pdf (Accessed 1st August 2014).

Department for Children, Schools and Families (DCFS) (2009) *The Lamb Inquiry: Special Educational Needs and Parental Confidence*. Available at: webarchive.nationalarchives.gov.uk/20130401151715/https://www.education.gov.uk/publications/eOrderingDownload/01143-2009DOM-EN.pdf (Accessed 2nd February 2013).

Department for Education (DfE) (1994) *The code of practice on the identification and assessment of special educational needs*. London: HMSO.

Department for Education (DfE) (2012) *Support and Aspiration: A New Approach to Special Educational Needs and Disability*. Available at: www.gov.uk/government/uploads/system/uploads/attachment_data/file/198141/Support_and_Aspiration_Green-Paper-SEN.pdf (Accessed 15th March 2015).

Department for Education (DfE) (2014a) *Parents Feel More Supported Ahead of Radical SEND Reforms*. [Press Release]. 15th August 2014. Available at: www.gov.uk/government/news/parents-feel-more-supported-ahead-of-radical-send-reforms (Accessed 1st September 2014).

Department for Education (DfE) (2014b) *National Curriculum in England: Framework for Key Stages 1 to 4*. Available at: www.gov.uk/government/publications/national-curriculum-in-england-frame

work-for-key-stages-1-to-4/the-national-curriculum-in-england-framework-for-key-stages-1-to-4 (Accessed 4th September 2014).

Department for Education (DfE) and Department of Health (DoH) (2014) *Special Educational Needs and Disability Code of Practice: 0–25 years*. Available at: www.gov.uk/government/uploads/ system/uploads/attachment_data/file/342440/SEND_Code_of_Practice_approved_by_Parliament_ 29.07.14.pdf (Accessed 10th September 2014).

Department for Education (DfE) and Department of Health (DoH) (2015) *Special Educational Needs and Disability Code of Practice: 0–25 years*. Available at: www.gov.uk/government/uploads/ system/uploads/attachment_data/file/398815/SEND_Code_of_Practice_January_2015.pdf (Accessed 1st February 2015).

Department for Education and Skills (DfES) (2001) *Special Educational Needs Code of Practice*. Available at: webarchive.nationalarchives.gov.uk/20130401151715/www.education.gov.uk/publica tions/eOrderingDownload/0581-2001-SEN-CodeofPractice.pdf (Accessed 20th September 2014).

Office for Standards in Education (Ofsted) (2010) *The Special Educational Needs and Disability Review: A Statement is not Enough*. Available at: www.gov.uk/government/uploads/system/ uploads/attachment_data/file/413814/Special_education_needs_and_disability_review.pdf (Accessed 5th October 2015).

Parliament: House of Commons Education and Skills Committee (2006) *Special Educational Needs: Third Report of the Session 2005–06* (HC 478-1). London: The Stationery Office.

The SENCO role in policy and practice

Beginnings to present day

The Special Educational Needs and Disability (SEND) Code of Practice (DfE and DoH, 2015) (hereafter referred to as the SEND Code of Practice), published by the Department for Education and Department of Health (DfE and DoH), provides the statutory SEND guidance to schools in relation to the 2014 Children and Families Act. It is also the key document that every Special Educational Needs Coordinator (SENCO) needs to become familiar with. The SEND Code of Practice details all the key processes and duties for local authorities, health bodies, schools and colleges. In addition to this, from a SENCO's perspective, it is the guidance which explains the SENCO role, as well as the role of others, within their setting and further afield.

The SEND Code of Practice (DfE and DoH, 2015) is emphatic regarding the central purpose of the SENCO position within schools. The guidance states that the SENCO has responsibility for the coordination of specific SEN provision, but equally highlights the strategic nature of the role: 'The SENCO has an important role to play with the head teacher and governing body, in determining the strategic development of SEN policy and provision in the school' DfE and DoH, 2015, p. 106).

The SENCO role has been a statutory requirement within mainstream, state-funded schools for over 20 years. Yet despite the length of time the role has been in existence, defining the role and unpicking exactly what a SENCO does has proved, over time, to be difficult. It could be argued that part of the challenge with defining the role is due to its complex and diverse nature. However, differences between school settings, with different priorities, cultures and processes, also contribute to this disparity. Hallett and Hallett sum this up by stating that the position is 'as varied as the schools and settings in which the post-holders are employed, and the role is delivered' (2010, p. 1).

A further complexity is how the role has been perceived by others, including parents, teachers, senior leadership and external agencies. Research by Cole (2005, cited in Tissot, 2013) suggests that the SENCO role is one which is typically seen as low status and focused on operational tasks. Yet, as illustrated above, this view contrasts with the SEND Code of Practice (DfE and DoH, 2015) which states that the SENCO role should be involved with the strategic development of SEN policy and provision. However, it could also be argued that the SENCO role is not understood by senior leaders and colleagues

(Curran et al., 2018) and that tensions related to the role, for example widely reported issues with workload, may also feed into how others perceive the SENCO role in schools.

Given the lack of clarity regarding the SENCO role, it is perhaps unsurprising that one of the early challenges a new SENCO may face is trying to determine exactly what they should be doing and how they should be conducting their role. It could be argued that the SENCO role is one which has a great deal of responsibility – to ensure children and families are supported, provision is appropriate and that children make good progress. The SENCO is often viewed by staff as the *expert*, and this may be a perception which the new SENCO may initially feel uncomfortable with. Further challenges may relate to how they manage the role against competing priorities, a lack of seniority or a lack of time and/or resources, all of which have the potential to impact on not only the efficacy of the SENCO, but also their well-being.

The first chapter of this book explores the role of the SENCO and seeks to consider how the role has emerged and evolved over time. The nature of the role, in terms of the responsibilities as stated by the SEND Code of Practice (DfE and DoH, 2015), will subsequently be explored with the aim of providing SENCOs with a clear understanding of their role, as stated in current policy. The chapter will also consider how these responsibilities translate into practice and how this 'pivotal' role, as described by government guidance (DfES, 2004, p. 116), is enacted in school settings, with consideration given to the recent, additional regulations and policies which have impacted on the SENCO role. The chapter will encourage SENCOs to reflect on the nature of their role in their own setting and not only compare this to national guidance, but also consider how this relates to what is stated in their school policies. The chapter will conclude with a focus on how SENCOs can begin to shape their SENCO role and why this is important.

In summary, this chapter focuses on:

- the beginnings of the SENCO role;
- the SENCO role today: responsibilities as determined by the 2015 SEND Code of Practice;
- the SENCO role in practice; and
- shaping your SENCO role.

The beginnings of the SENCO role

It could be argued that the evolution of the SENCO role can be traced back to the Warnock Report (DES, 1978). The 1978 committee, led by Mary Warnock, were appointed by the then government to review educational provision for children with disabilities in England, Scotland and Wales. The culmination of this process was the publication of the Warnock Report (DES, 1978), which made a number of recommendations in relation to the education of children with additional needs. The report recommended that the focus should shift to prioritise the child's educational need, rather than their 'learning disability or impairment' (Hodkinson, 2016, p. 4). The term *Special Educational Needs* (SEN) was also recommended as new terminology; this term was later defined within the 1981 Education Act. Additionally, specific reference was made regarding the integration of children with SEN within mainstream schools and segregation, which was the accepted practice at the time, was criticised. Following the publication of the Warnock Report, and the subsequent 1981 Education Act, there was an increased commitment to the education of pupils with SEN within the 'ordinary' school (Norwich, 2010, p. 37). Therefore, it could be argued that the Warnock report was instrumental regarding the development of the inclusive schooling movement and, as a direct consequence, the development of the SENCO role.

The role of the SENCO was first formally introduced in the *Code of Practice on the Identification and Assessment of Special Educational Needs* (DfE, 1994, hereafter referred to as the 1994 Code) following the 1993 Education Act. This was the first piece of statutory central government guidance to local authorities and schools following the 1981 Education Act, Part III, which laid down the responsibilities for schools regarding children with SEN, specifically relating to mainstream educational provision for children with additional needs. The role of the SENCO was defined, and made statutory, through this legislation. The guidance placed a requirement on schools to appoint a named person in school as the SENCO. This requirement has remained in place ever since and was recently re-affirmed in the most recent statutory guidance; the SEND Code of Practice (DfE and DoH, 2015).

As such, it could be argued that it was the 1994 Code (DfE, 1994) which gave the SENCO role validity (Cowne, 2005). Mackenzie (2007), in agreement with Cowne, suggests that while many schools had already appointed a person to be responsible for children with SEN prior to 1994, this was the school's choice as opposed to a requirement.

How the SENCO role has evolved from 1994 to the present day

In 2001, the 1994 Code (DfE, 1994) was revised and replaced with the *Special Educational Needs Code of Practice* (DfES, 2001) (hereafter referred to as the 2001 Code). In part, the 2001 Code sought to address some of the issues which accompanied the introduction of the 1994 Code, in particular SENCO workload. However, whilst there were several key differences between the 1994 and 2001 Codes, the requirement to have a designated person appointed as the SENCO remained. The 2001 Code referred to the coordination of provision for children, liaising with parents and supporting staff, amongst other duties.

However, with regards to the SENCO role, a key change from the 1994 Code to the 2001 Code was the introduction of the term 'strategic' (DfES, 2001, p. 15). Day-to-day responsibility for the operation of the school's SEN policy remained, yet there was a clear expectation that the SENCO would work strategically with the head teacher and senior management team (SMT) when developing and planning for SEN provision within the school. It should also be noted that the 2001 Code introduced a new managerial aspect to the role, with suggested responsibility for 'overseeing' and 'managing learning support assistants' (DfES, 2001, p. 50).

2008: a changing landscape with the introduction of current SENCO regulations

In 2006, the House of Commons Education and Skills Committee report (*House of Commons Education and Skills report*) on SEN (2006) was published. The report was tasked with exploring the current SEN system, with specific consideration to its failings and how it could be improved. In line with earlier reports (Audit Commission, 2002; Warnock, 2005), it was through this report that concerns were formally expressed regarding SEN policy, specifically in relation to inclusion (Baker, 2007). Central to the concerns was the idea that policies and terminology were contradictory (House of Commons Education and Skills Committee, 2006). The report urged that the government should clarify its position on SEN, both regarding inclusion and strategic direction. A vision was required for the future with, potentially, an updated strategy and non-statutory guidance. The report further stated, 'Special Educational Needs should be prioritised, brought into the mainstream education policy agenda, and radically improved' (House of Commons Education and Skills Committee, 2006, p. 7).

The government responded to the House of Commons Education and Skills report (2006) and, in part, this response was later formalised through the SENCO regulations made in 2008 (with amendments in 2009). The regulations came into force on 1st September 2009 and remain in place today. This chapter will refer to the regulations as the 2008/2009 SENCO regulations. The requirements in this paragraph are that the SENCO:

* is a qualified teacher, the head teacher or the appointed acting head teacher;
* is required to complete an induction period under regulations made under section 19 of the Teaching and Higher Education Act 1998(a), has satisfactorily completed such an induction period; and

- is working as a teacher at the school.

(2008, pp. 1–2)

Up until the introduction of the SENCO regulations, the SENCO role had often been held by other members of staff within the school, including teaching assistants. The SENCO regulations addressed this through stating that:

(3) The requirement in this paragraph is that the SENCO is the head teacher or acting head teacher of the school and meets the requirements of regulations made under section 135 of the Education Act 2002 if required to do so(b).

(4) The requirements in this paragraph are that the SENCO— (a) has had responsibility for co-ordinating the making of special educational provision for pupils with special educational needs at the school for a period of at least six months ending on the 31st August 2009, and (b) the governing body is satisfied that— (i) the SENCO is taking steps to meet the requirements in paragraph (2), and (ii) there is a reasonable prospect that the SENCO will meet those requirements by 1st September 2011.

(2009, p. 2)

The regulations further stated that it is the responsibility of the governing body to determine the leadership and management nature of the role, in relation to the rest of the school.

The 2008/2009 SENCO regulations gave further specific guidance regarding the SENCO role. In addition, it is the responsibility of the governing body to determine the key responsibilities for the SENCO and monitor the effectiveness of the SENCO in undertaking those responsibilities.

The SENCO regulations went on to unpick this further, stating:

The key responsibilities [of the SENCO] referred to in paragraph (1) may include the carrying out, or arranging for the carrying out, of the following tasks –

(a) in relation to each of the registered pupils whom the SENCO considers may have special educational needs, informing a parent of the pupil that this may be the case as soon as is reasonably practicable;

(b) in relation to each of the registered pupils who have special educational needs –

    (i) identifying the pupil's special educational needs,

    (ii) co-ordinating the making of special educational provision for the pupil which meets those needs,

    (iii) monitoring the effectiveness of any special educational provision made for the pupil,

    (iv) securing relevant services for the pupil where necessary,

(v) ensuring that records of the pupil's special educational needs and the special educational provision made to meet those needs are maintained and kept up to date,

(vi) liaising with and providing information to a parent of the pupil on a regular basis about that pupil's special educational needs and the special educational provision being made for those needs,

(vii) ensuring that, where the pupil transfers to another school or educational institution, all relevant information about the pupil's special educational needs and the special educational provision made to meet those needs is conveyed to the governing body or (as the case may be) the proprietor of that school or institution, and

(viii) promoting the pupil's inclusion in the school community and access to the school's curriculum, facilities and extra-curricular activities;

(c) selecting, supervising and training learning support assistants who work with pupils who have special educational needs;

(d) advising teachers at the school about differentiated teaching methods appropriate for individual pupils with special educational needs;

(e) contributing to in-service training for teachers at the school to assist them to carry out the tasks referred to in paragraph (b);

(f) preparing and reviewing the information required to be published by the governing body pursuant to the Education (Special Educational Needs) (Information) (England) Regulations 1999(a), the objectives of the governing body in making provision for special educational needs, and the special educational needs policy referred to in paragraph 1 of Schedule 1 to those Regulations.

(2009, pp. 2–3)

Something to think about

In relation to the 2008/2009 SENCO regulations, listed above:

- Who has determined your SENCO role at school?
- What input has your governing body had in terms of determining your role as a SENCO?

The amendments in 2009 introduced one of the biggest changes to the SENCO role which has directly impacted on workload – the introduction of the national accreditation for Special Educational Needs Coordinators (SENCOs) now commonly known as the National Award for SEN Coordination (NA SENCO).

The introduction of the National Award for Special Educational Needs Coordination

The 2008/2009 SENCO regulations stated that, from 1st September 2009, any newly appointed SENCO, or any SENCO who has been in the post for less than twelve months, must achieve the 'National Award in Special Educational Needs Co-ordination [NA SENCO] within three years of appointment' (DfE and DoH, 2015, p. 108). The stated aim of introducing the award was to ensure that the SENCO has the necessary skills, knowledge and authority to undertake the role within the school.

The NA SENCO is a postgraduate qualification that must be at least 60 credits at Level 7 (Masters degree level). In addition to this, SENCOs must demonstrate that they have met the nationally set Learning Outcomes (NCTL, 2014). The NA SENCO is delivered by a provider, which must be affiliated to a Higher Education Institute to award the Masters level credits. This means that the provider is often, but not always, a university. The award can be delivered in a variety of ways, including face-to-face and online sessions, depending on the provider. The chapter on 'Managing your role' (Chapter 7) will consider SENCO well-being and will also specifically consider how to pace yourself through the NA SENCO.

- Find out more about the NA SENCO and read the Register of Quality Providers: www.nasen.org.uk/about/partnerships/.
- Find out more about the NA SENCO Learning Outcomes: https://assets. publishing.service.gov.uk/government/uploads/system/uploads/attach ment_data/file/354172/nasc-learning-outcomes-final.pdf.

The SENCO role today: responsibilities as determined by the 2015 SEND Code of Practice

2014 was a crucial year in the realm of SEN with the introduction of the 2014 (now 2015) SEND Code of Practice (DfE and DoH, 2015). The current SEND Code of Practice, as per previous versions, outlines the key responsibilities which may be part of the SENCO role. To a degree, there has been a review of the SENCO role within the SEND Code of Practice, but the changes are relatively subtle. Some of the key points from the 2001 Code (DfES, 2001) remain, however, there are some key differences. The SEND Code of Practice (DfE and DoH, 2015) states that the responsibilities may include the following (new/amended responsibilities from the previous 2001 Code (DfES, 2001) have been highlighted in italics):

- Overseeing the day-to-day operation of the school's SEN policy.
- Coordinating provision for children with SEN.
- *Liaising with the relevant Designated Teacher where a looked after pupil has SEN.*
- *Advising on the graduated approach to providing SEN support.*
- Advising on the deployment of the school's delegated budget and other resources to meet pupils' needs effectively.
- Liaising with parents of pupils with SEN.
- Liaising with early years providers, other schools, educational psychologists, health and social care professionals, and independent or voluntary bodies.
- *Being a key point of contact with external agencies, especially the local authority and its support services.*
- *Liaising with potential next providers of education to ensure a pupil and their parents are informed about options and a smooth transition is planned.*
- *Working with the head teacher and school governors to ensure that the school meets its responsibilities under the Equality Act (2010) with regard to reasonable adjustments and access arrangements.*
- *Ensuring that the school keeps the records of all pupils with SEN up to date.*

(DfE and DoH, 2015, pp. 108–109)

Something to think about

- Read pages 108–109 in the SEND Code of Practice to find out more about the SENCO role.
- Read your school SEN policy – what does it say about your role?
- Read your SEN information report – what does it say about your role?
- How do the three documents compare?

The SEND Code of Practice (DfE and DoH, 2015) introduced some key changes which are reflective of the implementation of the 2014 Children and Families Act. These include the introduction of the graduated approach, the four part cycle of Assess, Plan, Do and Review – which seeks to create a systematic approach to identifying needs, planning provision and revisiting decisions – as well as facilitating a more detailed and collaborative approach to identifying and supporting children with SEN. It is notable that the outlined responsibilities state that the SENCO is an advisor, rather than someone who takes a more instrumental role, echoing the key principle of the SEND Code of Practice that every teacher is responsible for all children in their class, including those with SEN. However, some of the changes may be described as more subtle. For example, the SENCO's responsibilities may include liaising with the designated teacher for looked after children. Whilst this is seemingly innocuous, it may be reflective of how the SENCO role is developing to include wider responsibilities beyond that of SEN; for example, recent research has illustrated how the SENCO role is growing to incorporate more vulnerable groups (Curran et al., 2018).

As well as noting the additions to the SENCO responsibilities within the SEND Code of Practice (DfE and DoH, 2015), it is notable that some aspects of the 2001 (DfES, 2001) Code have been omitted. These include:

- Liaising with and advising fellow teachers (replaced with 'provides professional guidance to colleagues') (DfE and DoH, 2015, p. 108).
- Managing learning support assistants.
- Contributing to the in-service training of staff.

It could also be argued that the SEND Code of Practice (DfE and DoH, 2015) suggests a broader view of provision, and potentially indicates a move away from the idea that teaching assistants automatically have a direct role to play when supporting children with SEN, a role which historically has had significant responsibility for providing support both in and out of the classroom (Blatchford et al., 2009). However, it is clear in the SEND Code of Practice that a broader view has been taken with regards to support, with direct reference to the SENCO's responsibility for provision, budgets and resources, rather than the management of teaching assistants.

Finally, it could also be argued that the strategic nature of the role has been emphasised within the SEND Code of Practice (DfE and DoH, 2015), with a focus on the SENCO as a point of contact and one of liaison, suggesting coordination and leadership. The 2001 Code stated that many schools found it 'effective' if the SENCO was part of the senior leadership team (SLT) (DfES, 2001, p. 51). This is echoed in the SEND Code of Practice: 'They [the SENCO] will be most effective in that role if they are part of the school leadership team' (DfE and DoH, 2015, p. 108). However, this is not always the case, with a recent survey of SENCOs suggesting that only 50% of SENCOs, and only 22% of secondary SENCOs, were on the SLT due to their SENCO role (Curran et al., 2018). As such, Chapter 3 explores the idea of SENCO leadership and considers how SENCOs can be effective leaders whether or not they are part of the SLT.

The SENCO role in practice

Part of the challenge of being a new SENCO is understanding exactly what you should be doing in practice, where to even begin! As a new SENCO it is important to gather some key information as soon as you start the role.

The new SENCO checklist

- Read the chapter in the SEND Code of Practice (DfE and DoH, 2015) which is relevant to your setting.
- Read your school SEN policy.
- Read your school SEN information report.
- Find out who your SEN governor is and make links.
- Find out how much time you have allocated to the role each week.
- Find out who can support you with administration.
- Find out who is on your SEN register.
- Check which children have Education, Health and Care (EHC) plans and find out when their reviews are due.
- Locate where records are stored.
- Note any key children who are current concerns. Find out actions to date.
- Make links with the local authority.
- Find out if there is a SENCO cluster group in your area.
- Find out who your Looked After Children Coordinator is.
- Look at wider support such as nasen www.nasen.org.uk and the SEND Gateway.

Once you have this information it is important to unpick the responsibilities as detailed in the SEND Code of Practice (DfE and DoH, 2015) and work out what these mean in your role. For example, the SEND Code of Practice states that the SENCO should be 'overseeing the day-to-day operation of the school's SEN policy' (DfE and DoH, 2015, p. 108). In practice, this may mean that the SENCO has a key role in ensuring appropriate support and access to the curriculum for children with SEN, although s/he may not necessarily be involved in the practical implementation of this (Griffiths and Dubsky, 2012). Certainly a key aspect of the role is reactive (Rosen-Webb, 2011). This suggests a multi-faceted proactive and reactive role. These descriptions reflect the SEND Code of Practice (DfE and DoH, 2015) in that the SENCO is someone who advises but does not necessarily directly act, for example by teaching pupils with SEN. However, what are the specific activities which a SENCO does?

Types of SENCO activities

Whilst the role of the SENCO, in practice, is broad and different in every context, there will be some key activities which are relevant to almost all settings.

Note – this list is not exhaustive and is in no particular order, but will give you an idea of what a SENCO does on a daily, weekly, monthly, termly and yearly basis!

- Making sure records and data are up to date.
- Ensuring at the start of the year that all staff have the correct information regarding children who have additional needs in their classes and what strategies and provision they need in place.
- Being available to support and advise staff as they work through the four part cycle of Assess, Plan, Do and Review, known as the graduated approach. This includes ensuring that there are systems in place regarding how the approach works in your school, advising and signposting staff on strategies and interventions to support children in their lessons and supporting teachers with reviewing pupils' targets and progress (see Chapter 5, 'Leading and supporting colleagues').
- Timetabling support and interventions for pupils.
- Monitoring the effectiveness of the additional support in place.
- Reviewing provision across the school, identifying gaps and resource needs.
- Conducting data analysis to identify needs, requirements for provision, progress of pupils, specific groups or trends which may indicate a need for short- or more longer-term support.
- Carrying out observations and assessments of children to support staff in developing their provision, strategies and/or gathering further evidence of need.
- Monitoring and advising on planning and assessment.
- Paperwork! Completing referrals, requests for a needs assessment, annual review paperwork or requests for additional support.
- Liaising with the local authority.
- Liaising with parents – raising or responding to concerns, working together to determine support.
- Liaising with other schools to determine transition arrangements for children.
- Liaising with external agencies to arrange assessments, visits and reviews. Arranging time to work with the pupil and meet with the teacher. Facilitation of discussions regarding support and next steps between all parties, including the pupil and parents.
- Meetings! With pupils, parents and external agencies. These may be informal meetings with parents sharing concerns or follow-ups from external agency involvement, or more formal meetings to determine next steps or conduct an annual review, for example.
- Responding to immediate pupil needs/crisis.
- Auditing staff needs regarding additional support and/or continuing professional development (CPD).
- Management of teaching assistants.
- Creating support for teachers through delivering training or providing materials in specific areas of SEN.
- Supporting and mentoring new staff.

- Reviewing the SEN policy and SEN information report.
- Reviewing the strategic development of SEN across the school, including identifying any areas for development, for example parental participation.
- Learning walks with a specific focus on an area of development.
- Meetings with the SEN governor to inform them of current issues and priorities for development.

Something to think about

- How do the bullet points above relate to the responsibilities as outlined in the SEND Code of Practice (DfE and DoH, 2015)?
- Which of these activities would need to be done on a daily, weekly, monthly, termly and yearly basis in your setting?
- Have a look at nasen and the SEND Gateway for further information on developing a SENCO annual calendar.
- www.nasen.org.uk
- www.sendgateway.org.uk/

Shaping your SENCO role

Starting out as a new SENCO, either new to a school or brand new to the role, can be daunting as there is so much to learn and you may be trying to work out exactly what you should be doing. However, as stated earlier, every school is different and therefore every SENCO role is different. Therefore, whilst there may be commonality between SENCO roles, there is also difference in how the role is executed; every SENCO will have their own priorities and their own approaches. To begin to explore this for yourself can be a great opportunity as you can begin to shape the role and determine the SENCO that you want to be. Not only will this help you be clear regarding your SENCO role, but it will help others understand your role, as well as their own. It is therefore even more important that SENCOs seek to establish their role, and to ensure that this is clearly communicated to all those they work with.

Something to think about

Having looked at the SEND Code of Practice, your school policy and SEN information report, you are probably beginning to shape an idea of how the

SENCO role looks in your school. You might have identified key responsibilities you were not aware of, or areas you would like to focus on.

So far, what do you spend most of your time doing?

- Teaching intervention groups?
- Firefighting/problem solving?
- Advising teachers?
- Managing staff?

This list is not exhaustive. However, have a think about what you spend most of your time doing. In terms of how you see your role developing, what are the key areas you need to develop? You can begin to use the identification of these ideas to shape your role.

Keep this information to one side. Later in the book we will be looking at your priorities for SEN and inclusion in your school. We will then look at what is helping and what is hindering you in fulfilling those actions.

It is relevant to note that the role of SENCO is often one given in addition to the responsibility of class or subject teacher, or deputy head (Rosen-Webb, 2011), which will impact on how you are effectively able to carry out and shape your SENCO role. Time issues are explored in Chapter 7, 'Managing your role'.

As a SENCO it is important to think about your SENCO role and to be clear as to what you should be doing, particularly if your time is limited. This may change over time as you respond to differing priorities, however clarity is a helpful starting point. Later in the book we will look at how to identify and set out priorities through a SEN development plan.

Ideas in action

Anna was appointed to the SENCO role after the previous school SENCO retired. She was immediately enrolled on the NA SENCO at a provider close to her school. At the first session, the course leader asked the SENCOs to read through their school SEN policy, the SEN information report and pages 108 and 109 of the SEND Code of Practice (DfE and DoH, 2015). In groups, the SENCOs had to compare the three documents and think about:

- their role and what they thought they would be doing as a SENCO;

- what the school SEN policy and SEN information report said about the SENCO role;
- what the SEND Code of Practice said about the responsibilities of the SENCO role; and
- how the three documents inter-relate.

Anna had only been in the role for a few weeks, so it was difficult to reflect on her role. Instead, she thought about what she had anticipated she would be doing when she took the role on, but also what she had seen the previous SENCO do.

She was surprised to see that the school policy talked about wider responsibilities as well as directly teaching groups of children, but did not talk about strategic leadership. Anna discussed this with her course leader as she felt that to embed her role, and the SEN policy, within school it was important to address these areas.

Anna decided that she would arrange a time to review her role with the head teacher in the first instance to share with them the information from the NA SENCO, using it is as a starting point for discussion. This also happened to coincide with the time that the SEN policy needed reviewing. Anna felt that as a new SENCO she could use both the NA SENCO and the SEN policy as vehicles through which she could shape her role within school.

Note: It is also useful to think about the role of the SEN governor here. It may be helpful to liaise with them regarding your role, so they can advocate for you and your role.

In summary

Hopefully this chapter has given you a brief overview of how the SENCO role has developed over time. Through using the SEND Code of Practice (DfE and DoH, 2015), as well as your school SEN policy and SEN information report, you will begin to understand your role in your setting. You will begin to identify how you are spending your time, but also the areas that you need to focus on in relation to what is expected, by both your school but also statutory guidance. The whole-school ethos towards SEN and inclusion, as well as your SENCO priorities, will also determine your SENCO role. The next chapter in the book will explore how to shape your role as a leader of SEN through developing your understanding of inclusion and SEN in your school, all of which will help further shape your SENCO role as well as develop inclusive practice in your setting.

References

Audit Commission. (2002) *Special educational needs: A mainstream issue.* Available at: www.ttrb3.org.uk/audit-commission-special-educational-needs-a-mainstream-issue/ (Accessed 4th May 2016).

Baker, J. (2007) 'The British government's strategy for SEN: Implications for the role and future development of special schools', *Support for Learning*, 22 (2), pp. 72–77.

Blatchford, P., Bassett, P., Brown, P. and Webster, R. (2009) 'The effect of support staff on pupil engagement and individual attention', *British Educational Research Journal*, 35 (5), pp. 661–686.

Children and Families Act 2014, ch. 6. Available at: www.legislation.gov.uk/ukpga/2014/6/pdfs/ukpga_20140006_en.pdf (Accessed 1st August 2014).

Cowne, E. (2005) *The SENCO handbook: Working within a whole-school approach.* 5th edn. Abingdon, UK: David Fulton.

Curran, H., Moloney, H., Heavey, A. and Boddison, A. (2018) *It's about time: The impact of SENCO workload on the professional and the school.* Available at: www.bathspa.ac.uk/schools/education/research/senco-workload/ (Accessed 3rd January 2019).

Department for Education (DfE). (1994) *The Code of Practice on the identification and assessment of special educational needs.* London: HMSO.

Department for Education (DfE) and Department of Health (DoH). (2015) *Special educational needs and disability Code of Practice: 0–25 years.* Available at: www.gov.uk/government/uploads/system/uploads/attachment_data/file/398815/SEND_Code_of_Practice_January_2015.pdf (Accessed 1st February 2015).

Department for Education and Skills (DfES). (2001) *Special educational needs Code of Practice.* Available at: webarchive.nationalarchives.gov.uk/20130401151715/www.education.gov.uk/publications/eOrderingDownload/0581-2001-SEN-CodeofPractice.pdf (Accessed 20th September 2014).

Department for Education and Skills (DfES). (2004) *Removing barriers to achievement: The government's strategy for special educational needs.* Available at: webarchive.nationalarchives.gov.uk/20130401151715/www.education.gov.uk/publications/standard/publicationDetail/Page1/DfES%200117%202004 (Accessed 1st July 2016).

Department of Education and Science (DES). (1978) *Special educational needs: Report of the committee of enquiry into the education of handicapped children and young people.* Available at: www.educationengland.org.uk/documents/warnock/warnock1978.html (Accessed 30th September 2014).

Education Act 1981, ch. 60. Available at: www.legislation.gov.uk/ukpga/1981/60/pdfs/ukpga_19810060_en.pdf (Accessed 5th July 2016).

Education Act 1993, ch. 35. Available at: www.legislation.gov.uk/ukpga/1993/35/pdfs/ukpga_19930035_en.pdf (Accessed 5th July 2016).

Griffiths, D. and Dubsky, R. (2012) 'Evaluating the impact of the new National Award for SENCOs: Transforming landscapes or gardening in a gale?', *British Journal of Special Education*, 39 (4), pp. 164–172.

Hallett, F. and Hallett, G. (eds.) (2010) *Transforming the role of the SENCO: Achieving the National Award for SEN coordination.* Maidenhead, UK: Oxford University Press.

Hodkinson, A. (2016) *Key issues in special educational needs and inclusion.* London: Sage.

Mackenzie, S. (2007) 'A review of recent developments in the role of the SENCO in the UK', *British Journal of Special Education*, 34 (4), pp. 212–218.

National College of Teaching and Learning. (2014) *National Award for special educational needs co-ordination: Learning outcomes*. Available at: www.gov.uk/government/uploads/system/uploads/attachment_data/file/354172/nasc-learning-outcomes-final.pdf (Accessed 1st September 2014).

Norwich, B. (2010) 'Can we envisage the end of special educational needs? Has special educational needs outlived its usefulness?', *Psychology of Education Review*, 34 (2), pp. 13–21.

Parliament: House of Commons Education and Skills Committee. (2006) *Special educational needs: Third report of the session 2005–06*. (HC 478-1). London: The Stationery Office.

Rosen-Webb, S. (2011) 'Nobody tells you how to be a SENCO', *British Journal of Special Education*, 38 (4), pp. 159–168.

The Education (Special Educational Needs Co-ordinators) (England) Regulations 2008 (SI 2008/ 2945). Available at: http://dera.ioe.ac.uk/10702/4/SI%202008%201945.pdf (Accessed 14th September 2013).

The Education (Special Educational Needs Co-ordinators) (England) (Amendment) Regulations 2009 (SI 2009/ 1387). Available at: http://dera.ioe.ac.uk/10702/5/uksi_20091387_en.pdf (Accessed 14th September 2013).

Tissot, C. (2013) 'The role of SENCOs as leaders', *British Journal of Special Education*, 40 (1), pp. 33–40.

Warnock, M. (2005) *Special education needs: A new look*. London: Continuum.

The SENCO as a leader
Your role, your school, your ethos

The SENCO role holds an interesting position within the broader structure of school leadership. It is a role which, by its very nature, is senior and is one which requires leadership. The leadership role can occur not only across the immediate school but, potentially, across a multi-academy trust as well as within wider networks; a key aspect related to leadership is the development of effective working practices with colleagues, parents and external agencies, amongst others.

As with the previous chapter, when considering the nature of the role in terms of leadership it can be helpful to go back to the statutory guidance. The *SEND Code of Practice* states, 'The SENCO has an important role to play with the head teacher and governing body, in determining the strategic development of SEN policy and provision in the school' in addition to, 'The SENCO has day-to-day responsibility for the operation of SEN policy and coordination of specific provision made to support individual pupils with SEN, including those who have Education, Health and Care (EHC) plans' (DfE and DoH, 2015, p. 108). Both statements infer that this is a senior position within schools. Equally, as the previous chapter explored, whilst the responsibilities of the SENCO role are broad there is a central focus on supporting colleagues and providing guidance, as well as developing capacity within teams and ensuring appropriate provision for children with SEN through family collaboration.

The SENCO role has often been divided into the operational and strategic aspects of the role, with the former focusing on the day to day, and the latter seeking to consider SEN provision in a more developmental sense across the whole school (Griffiths and Dubsky, 2012). However, whilst the role can be discussed in these terms, both aspects inter-relate and both require ongoing leadership (Rosen-Webb, 2011).

When considering both the operational and strategic aspects of the role, an identified barrier to executing these roles effectively has been the lack of seniority or status attached to the SENCO role (Pearson, 2008). It has been argued that primarily this is because the SENCO role is not required to be part of the senior leadership team (SLT). Whilst the SEND Code of Practice states 'They [the SENCO] will be most effective in that role if they are part of the school leadership team' (DfE and DoH, 2015, p. 108), it stops short of stating that this is a statutory requirement, despite this being a recommendation by the House of Commons Education And Skills Committee

(2006). As such, this has led to varied practice in schools and, it could be argued, has made it difficult for some SENCOs who are not part of the SLT to create meaningful change, at either an operational or strategic level, in their settings.

However, leadership is not all about being part of the SLT in school. Therefore, this chapter will seek to explore the leadership nature of the SENCO role in a broader sense. It will initially consider the difference between operational and strategic leadership before considering the underpinning factors which will influence the approach you take with your leadership, including your ethos towards inclusion and SEN, and what you consider to be good, inclusive practice. The chapter will then challenge you to consider what you want inclusion to look like in your school. The intention is that this will then lead you to think about the priorities, both operationally and strategically, that you wish to focus on in your school, which in turn will begin to shape how you lead this key area.

The SENCO role and its relationship to the SLT has long been debated (Szwed, 2007a; Oldham and Radford, 2011; Tissot, 2013). As such, the following chapter will also explore this issue and consider the impact being on the SLT can have on the SENCO role, and what to do if you are not part of the SLT.

In summary, this chapter focuses on:

- the SENCO as a leader: should I be operational, strategic or both?;
- leading on what? Developing and understanding your ethos towards inclusion;
- leading on what? Developing your understanding of the definition of SEN; and
- setting longer-term, strategic priorities.

The SENCO as a leader: should I be operational, strategic or both?

The SENCO role, and whether it sits within the school structure as middle or senior leadership, can be discussed and debated. However, it can certainly be argued that an effective SENCO is a necessary part of the team to enable a school community to develop an inclusive agenda (Tissot, 2013), and that true leadership is demonstrated when cultural, rather than structural, change has been achieved (Szwed, 2007b). The notion that the SENCO is an integral member of the school is echoed in law, with the Children and Families Act 2014 stating that state-funded schools must have a named individual as the SENCO, and the 2009 SENCO regulations further stating that the SENCO must be employed by the school as a teacher and hold qualified teacher status (QTS). If required, depending on their circumstances, the SENCO must hold the

National Award for SEN Coordination (NA SENCO). This, to an extent, illustrates the importance of the role – at least in legislation.

The notion of the SENCO as a leader is problematic, in part because there are so many factors which may impact on the efficacy of the SENCO role. Factors may include whether the SENCO is part of the SLT, whether they have good management support, sufficient resources allocated in terms of time and administrative support, as well as the attitudes of those who work with the SENCO. However, in addition to the issues related to seniority and support, a further issue may be the confusion regarding what the SENCO should be leading on and whether their role should be operational, strategic or both; an issue compounded due to the differing contexts of individual schools.

To help us understand why the SENCO is often discussed in operational and strategic terms, it is useful to look back at how the role developed in the first instance. When the role was first established, it signified for many teachers an immediate move from SEN teacher to SEN manager (Garner, 1996). This illustrated a crucial shift for SENCOs as it was often the case that the specialist SEN teacher became the SENCO (Derrington, 1997). Certainly, as the role developed, it appeared there was a difficulty balancing contact with pupils and the management of the responsibilities (Bowers et al., 1998).

Yet, the early incarnation of the role was expected to incorporate a managerial aspect, as well as maintaining time supporting and teaching children with SEN, perhaps illustrating the first foray towards a more strategic element to the role. Many SENCOs, and it could be argued colleagues, saw the element of providing specialist support as important (Cowne, 2005). Following the introduction of the 2001 Code (DfES, 2001), concerns were raised as to whether it was possible to develop the role strategically; it was already a stretched role. The 2001 Code, however, was clear that the SENCO 'should be closely involved in the strategic development of the SEN policy and provision' (DfES, 2001, p.11), a point further emphasised in the most recent SEND Code of Practice (DfE and DoH, 2015). Equally, since this point, it could be argued that greater accountability measures in the respect of inclusion, progress and school agendas, such as whether provision provides value for money, has made it imperative for the SENCO to develop the strategic side of their role to ensure that they have influence in their setting (Tissot, 2013).

So, what does this mean for new and current SENCOs? Perhaps the easiest way to explain the difference between the terms operational and strategic is to use a time frame. The operational side of the SENCO role will be more short-term focused, exploring what needs to happen and when, focusing on the day to day 'doing' of SEN provision. However, the strategic side of the SENCO role will be more forward-looking to the longer term. The strategic SENCO will be considering and identifying priorities for development within the wider school, through identifying how provision can be changed and developed over the longer term in their setting. The suggestion is that a strategic role is one which influences whole-school practices (Griffiths and Dubsky, 2012).

The idea of strategic practice is expanded a little further in the SEND Code of Practice (DfE and DoH, 2015) which refers to provision mapping and data as strategic tools to develop provision in schools. Such tools can be used to identify needs and training, as well as impact, which in turn can be used to identify priorities and related activities to improve the school offer.

Something to think about

Earlier in the book, you were asked to make a list, or think about, what you spend most of your time doing.

Have a look at the list and divide it into operational and strategic.

Is there a bias towards one aspect? Why do you think this is?

It is perhaps unsurprising that the majority of SENCOs may find that they are typically focused on carrying out operational responsibilities. The day to day cannot be ignored. In fact, a recent survey of over 1900 SENCOs found that 71% ranked 'administrative duties' as the tasks which took up most of their time in a week (Curran et al., 2018). Administrative tasks included activities such as completing referrals, annual review paperwork and making phone calls. However, research has shown that overly focusing on operational duties means that influence at a decision-making level is minimal (Shuttleworth, 2000 cited in Szwed, 2007b). This is supported by Griffiths and Dubsky (2012), who suggested that SENCOs often experienced frustration at the lack of opportunity to engage with strategic opportunities – again, we can hypothesise that the lack of opportunity may come from barriers related to time and leadership opportunities.

However, interestingly, the lack of opportunities to be strategic were also linked to the perception of the SENCO role by their colleagues, which Griffiths and Dubsky refer to as 'ground level managers – gardeners' (2012, p. 165). This suggests that how the role is viewed in school by colleagues is important when it comes to SENCOs having the *opportunity* to influence in a strategic manner. As a consequence, it can be frustrating for SENCOs who find themselves in a cycle of 'firefighting' rather than having adequate opportunity to develop the strategic elements of the role (Layton, 2005), as this may be how colleagues then continually perceive them. The inference here is that strategic opportunities need to be created, and embraced, to develop this aspect of the role; these opportunities will not develop on their own.

Something to think about

Have a look back at your list of operational and strategic activities. Focus on the 'operational' activities. Can you rank these in order of time? What do you spend most of your time focused on?

Ask yourself:

- Should I be doing this? Whose responsibility is this? Refer to the earlier chapter 'The SENCO role in policy and practice' (Chapter 2), as well as the SEND Code of Practice (DfE and DoH, 2015).
- What do you spend most of your time doing? Focus on the outcome of the activities you spend most of your time doing.
- What would you need to rebalance your activities to incorporate more strategy?

News flash: you have to be both!

Essentially, the SENCO role must incorporate both elements – operational and strategic (Rosen-Webb, 2011; Morewood, 2012). The SEND Code of Practice (DfE and DoH, 2015) and the revised NA SENCO Learning Outcomes (NCTL, 2014) also echo this point. Tissot (2013) suggests that best practice does not separate operational and strategic elements; the conflicting and competing elements need to co-exist within the one role. Certainly, more time allocated to the role would help SENCOs effectively address both these aspects – we will explore this later in the book. However, it is also important to consider how we focus on activities and whether there are recurring themes which we can address in a more strategic manner.

Ideas in action

Administration/paperwork was highlighted as a key issue with the National SENCO Workload Survey (Curran et al., 2018), however, it is important to think about how paperwork can be both a curse and a blessing, and how you can make it work for you.

Operational issue:

The requirement to complete various sets of annual review paperwork for various local authorities, due to the school's location which borders several local authorities.

Strategic solution:

Liaise with the local authority to explain the issue and query the legal necessity to complete 'their' version of the paperwork. Return to the SEND Code of Practice (DfE and DoH, 2015) and develop your own paperwork which you can use for every child, which incorporates all required elements, regardless of which local authority issued the Education, Health and Care plan.

Operational issue:

78% of SENCOs who responded to the National SENCO Workload Survey (Curran et al., 2018) stated that 'other roles/tasks often pull me away from being able to carry out the SENCO role'. SENCOs frequently referred to being called to support colleagues with the behaviour of children.

Strategic solution:

Identify the frequency with which you are being called away to support teachers with managing and supporting children's behaviour. Identify what does not get done as a result, and how this links to the school's statutory responsibilities regarding SEN. This is evidence to show the impact of being drawn away to other, non SEN-related, activities.

Does this indicate a training need related to supporting children's behaviour? Or a resource need in terms of personnel? This could equally indicate that a greater understanding of the SENCO role is required of colleagues. Share your thoughts with your SLT and build in a programme of action which addresses the most pressing issue, for example pastoral support 'on call', drawing upon the wider SLT rather than solely the SENCO.

Leading on what? Developing and understanding your ethos towards inclusion

The terms 'SEN' and 'inclusion' are both used frequently within education, yet how often do we stop to consider what they mean? As a leader of SEN it is important to consider your own understanding and ethos, as your interpretation of these terms may differ from a teacher down the corridor. Therefore, if you are discussing 'developing an inclusive environment' with staff, in a strategic sense, or, at a more operational level, considering whether an individual 'may have special educational needs', how do you know you are talking about the same thing?

Something to think about

One of the first things we ask our new SENCOs to do, as they begin the NA SENCO, is to consider and debate their understanding of inclusion and SEN. Think about:

- what the terms SEN and inclusion mean to you;
- what your aspirations are for the children and young people in your school, and how this relates to your vision of inclusion in your school; and
- whether you think that your vision is similar to that of your colleagues', pupils' and parents'.

It might be helpful to note that the *National Curriculum Inclusion Statement* cites:

> A wide range of pupils have special educational needs, many of whom also have disabilities. Lessons should be planned to ensure that there are no barriers to every pupil achieving. In many cases, such planning will mean that these pupils will be able to study the full national curriculum.
>
> (DfE and DoH, 2015, p. 94)

Have a look at your SEN policy and information report – what do these documents say about inclusion and does this reflect your ethos?

It could be argued that the Warnock Committee (DES, 1978) was instrumental regarding the beginning of the inclusive schooling movement. The 1978 committee report to the government, led by Warnock, introduced the term SEN and made a number of recommendations, which included making specific reference to the integration of children with SEN within mainstream schools. Whilst the practice of integration did not place requirements on schools to adapt learning, it undoubtedly acted as a precursor to the inclusive movement. Certainly, since Warnock and the subsequent 1981 Education Act, the term inclusion has undeniably gained greater traction within education.

However, the SEND Code of Practice does not state a definition of inclusion and no longer makes reference to the Centre of Studies for Inclusive Education (CSIE) Index for Inclusion (CSIE, 2014; DfE and DoH, 2015), although the term inclusion is referenced within the guidance. The SEND Code of Practice does make reference to the National Curriculum Inclusion Statement (DfE and DoH, 2015), which states that children should have access to a broad and balanced curriculum and sets three key areas of focus: learning challenges, responding to pupils' diverse learning needs, and overcoming barriers to learning and assessment for individuals and groups of pupils. This, however, does not define inclusion. Research literature has extensively explored the meaning and application of the term inclusion (Farrell, 2004; Avramidis and Norwich, 2016) and, whilst there is no singular agreement, it can prove to be a useful starting point.

Carrington and Elkins suggest that inclusion is greater than a practical review of approach, and as such, they hold the view that inclusion is '… a philosophy of acceptance where all pupils are valued and treated with respect' (2005, p. 86, cited in Glazzard et al., 2015, p. 24). The central premise of such an approach, as described by Ainscow (2006, cited in Ekins, 2012), is a school and system for all individuals. Glazzard and colleagues (2015) support the idea that the concept of inclusion relates to valuing all pupils and suggest that this relates closely to the original idea that Warnock (DES, 1978) was initially proposing. It is noteworthy, however, that Warnock (2005) later reported that inclusion should have an emphasis on the feeling of belonging; something that arguably has to come from the ethos of the school rather than a set of system changes. Perhaps this is where the role of the SENCO is key and has the opportunity to lead and advocate for the fundamental idea that all children belong.

From a practical perspective, inclusion can be defined as a school making a radical set of changes to ensure all children are embraced (Liasidou, 2012). However, this is not something which happens automatically but which needs to be systematically planned for. This enables the school to respond to the needs of the individual and therefore, as a consequence, provide equality of opportunity.

Certainly, when developing a shared understanding of the definition, rationale and associated aims of inclusion, government legislation and statutory guidance can play a key part in setting out the national tone for inclusion, as well as how this is enacted in schools. In terms of the SEND Code of Practice, inclusion relates to where children are educated, stating '[the] UK Government is committed to the inclusive education of disabled children and young people and the progressive removal of barriers to learning and participation in mainstream education' (DfE and DoH, 2015, p. 25). The concept of removing barriers and promoting access to learning potentially signifies a move away from a medical model of disability, where the difficulty is considered inherently within the child, to the idea that disability is socially created and comes as a result of the (inappropriate) environment. Adaptations must therefore be made within the environment, further highlighting the practical aspects of the inclusive model (Glazzard et al., 2015). It could be argued that the model reflected in the SEND Code of Practice is the social model of inclusion (Ainscow, 2007), in that it tasks local authorities, schools and teachers with identifying potential areas of difficulty and removing barriers. The SEND Code of Practice also states that, in most cases, planning will enable pupils to study the national curriculum (DfE, 2014).

Something to think about

Meeting children's needs is more than identifying individual next steps and considering how we can utilise resources to meet the targets. It is about considering the barriers presented within school and how these can be overcome. In some cases, this can be not only a 'quick win' situation but many students can benefit.

Pick one child in your school with identified SEN. Consider their specific needs and reflect on what, within your school environment, might pose a barrier (academic and social) to them accessing learning.

For example, consider a Year 8 child who is at a mainstream secondary school. You have observed that the pupil experiences sensory overload and finds break times particularly overwhelming. Things you can try:

- Notify all teachers that he can leave class 5 minutes early to avoid the rush in the corridors.
- Provide sensory breaks – a hall pass can provide this.
- Make sure all staff know the best place for the individual to be sat – at the back of the class, away from a window, for example?
- Create a quite space at breaktime, where children can go who need to be away from the 'hub-bub'.

Be strategic:

Are there any strategies you have identified which could be 'rolled out' as general good practice for supporting students with sensory needs?

Tensions with the inclusive model

As suggested above, it has been considered that one of the biggest tensions for inclusion relates to the pervading medical model of disability; the notion that the difficulty lies within the child (Thomas and Loxley, 2007). Such a model focuses on diagnosis and cures, thus prompting teachers and parents to look to external agencies, such as doctors, for advice and support (Hodkinson, 2016). This approach infers that the remit of SEN education is that of specialists, which in turn can shift the responsibility away from the teachers. This is directly at odds with the SEND Code of Practice (DfE and DoH, 2015). A move away from the medical model towards the social model of disability takes the emphasis away from the individual and centres it on the environment. This suggests that inclusion is everyone's responsibility, reflecting the accountability measures within the SEND Code of Practice (DfE and DoH, 2015). Yet, it could be argued that the current education system is entrenched in the two models of disability, thus promoting a conflict of inclusion policies.

As a SENCO you may find you have to strike a middle ground. Firstly, your environment needs to be considered – is it inclusive and from whose perspective? What are the potential barriers and how can these be removed? However, equally, there may be occasions where it is appropriate to move down a more diagnostic route. This can open avenues of support which previously were not accessible for the pupil and for parents; a 'diagnosis' can serve as a form of 'short hand'. It can provide teachers with a quick overview of the potential challenges a child might experience, and what they can do to support the individual in class. It could be argued that it is part of the SENCO role to ensure that there is a balance between these two aspects.

Something to think about

Think about a recent pupil who may have received a specific diagnosis, for example a child with dyslexia or a child on the autism spectrum. Think about how this has helped the child, the family and your colleagues. Also consider what some of the drawbacks might be. In your role as SENCO, how can you mitigate these? Can you add to the list below?

Advantages:

A greater understanding of the pupil's strengths and difficulties by those who work with them.
More targeted, specific provision.
Increased self-awareness for the pupil – a greater understanding of their own needs.

Disadvantages:

Mis-interpretation of pupil's needs by staff, due to a lack of understanding.
The pupil and family may feel overwhelmed.
Limited expectations.

SENCO considerations:

To consider staff training or support needs in a specific area.

Support with translating the report.
High expectations expected through the school ethos, demonstrated through targets.
Targeted pupil and family support, through direct SENCO input or signposting, or additional temporary provision for the pupil.

As a SENCO, you may find yourself advocating for pupils and parents in respect of moving forward towards a diagnosis. We will explore the role of the advocate later in the book.

The inclusive SENCO: being an advocate for inclusion

In addition to considering models of inclusion, which it could be argued is currently set between the two models of disability, it is important to consider how, as a SENCO, you can advocate for inclusion within your setting; an imperative aspect of being a leader. As a SENCO you may find that one way you can advocate for individuals is by challenging colleagues who may have lower expectations of children SEN or think that children with particular levels of need should not be placed in mainstream education. It is important to think about the removal of barriers to including all learners within the same community. However, it is also important to remember that definitions of community are broad and inclusion is not necessarily about being in a physical space. Therefore, conversely, you may find that you are in a position of advocating for the child to move to specialist provision, as is the request of the family. It is part of the SENCO role to champion the rights of the pupil.

Ideas in action

Have a look at the general activities on offer to all the individuals in your school, including school council, trips, clubs etc.

How inclusive are these activities? Remember, inclusion is more than offering activities and expecting the children to join in. How are sessions or activities actively made accessible? What are the potential barriers? It might be worthwhile to also think about representation. How are children with additional needs represented in various groups?

The overarching question is, 'how do we make all children, including those with special educational needs, feel like they are part of our school community?'

Finally, as a SENCO you may find that you specifically need to advocate for the inclusion of children with SEN in light of wider educational policy. Norwich suggests that the SEND system is 'interdependent' on the general educational system, which encompasses 'the National Curriculum and assessment, school inspection, the governance of schools and equality legislation' (2014, p. 404). This suggests that there are a number of external influencing factors which may impact on how successful a school is in its approach to inclusion. A number of educational policies are currently being critiqued in the media, primarily highlighting tensions between a 'policy for inclusion and a policy for the standards raising agenda' (Ellis and Tod, 2014, p. 2015). Perhaps this has most recently been identified through the practice of 'off-rolling', the practice where staff are encouraging pupils to move from the school at particular points during their education, namely because their specific needs may adversely impact on school data. The suggestion is that the inclusion agenda has been consistently undermined by the standards agenda, creating an impossible situation for schools. Perhaps this is one of the key areas where a SENCO can advocate for inclusion, particularly at secondary level. This is why clarity regarding inclusion, and what it means to you, is imperative.

In addition, there are further tensions we need to consider in relation to developing an inclusive ethos. It has been argued that to have one person solely responsible for SEN in a school is not inclusive (Layton, 2005; Oldham and Radford, 2011) and nor is it feasible, with Pearson suggesting that some viewed the role of the SENCO as 'retrogressive' (2010, p. 30). However, since the introduction of the SEND Code of Practice (DfE and DoH, 2015) there has been a move towards collective responsibility, with the SEND Code of Practice stating that all class/subject teachers have responsibility for all children in their class, including those with SEN. Yet, the role of the SENCO continues to be referred to in a singular sense (DfE and DoH, 2015). Later in the book we will explore how to develop a SEN team. However, one aspect of leadership is the unrelenting focus that SEN and inclusion is the business of everyone, and it is worth thinking about how you ensure that this message permeates all aspects of school.

Leading on what? Developing your understanding of the definition of SEN

As a SENCO, in addition to developing clarity regarding what we individually and collectively understand by the term inclusion, we also need to be clear regarding our understanding and application of the term SEN. A key part of leading as a SENCO is ensuring the wider understanding and consistent application of SEN as a legal definition across your setting. In contrast to the term inclusion, there is a legal definition of SEN. The 1981 Education Act adopted and legally defined the term 'SEN' as proposed by Warnock. The definition states that:

> A child has a SEN if he or she has a learning difficulty which calls for special educational provision to be made for him or her. A child has a learning difficulty if he or she:
>
> a. have a significantly greater difficulty in learning than the majority of children of the same age; OR
> b. have a disability which prevents or hinders them from making use of educational facilities of a kind generally provided for children of the same age in schools within the area of the local authority; OR
> c. are under compulsory school age and fall within the definition at a. or b. above or would do so if special educational provision was not made for them.
>
> (DfES, 2001: 6)

Whilst this aids our understanding, perhaps the issue for the SENCO, as a leader, is how the definition is interpreted in their setting. The SEND Code of Practice (DfE and DoH, 2015) is clear regarding the process for identification of SEN, and as such it is important that you and staff are familiar with this. Later in the book we will explore ways in which you can support colleagues, including how to support them in their understanding of this area. However, as a SENCO it is imperative that you know the processes in your setting for the identification, and subsequent support, of SEN.

Ideas in action

Neil is a new primary SENCO, currently on the National Award for SEN Coordination. He is clear regarding the legal definition of SEN, however is unclear as to how this is applied in his setting. As such he

---

- reviewed the SEN policy and SEN information report to see how it related to:
- the legal definition of SEN; and
- the graduated approach to identifying SEN in schools as outlined by the SEND Code of Practice.

Neil identified that there was some discrepancy. He brought together a small group of colleagues to ask them if the processes outlined in the documents reflected what they were doing. He then compared this with the school's documents and the statutory guidance. The SEN policy and information report were amended and then went to the appropriate individuals, including the governing body, for review.

Note

Parents, Ofsted and other interested parties will refer to your school documents to understand the processes for identifying and supporting SEN in your school. As a SENCO, and as a school leader, you need to ensure that the documents accurately reflect what is happening.

Tensions with the term SEN

Since the term SEN is defined in legal terms, it is perhaps surprising that it can be problematic in its practical application. However, one of the questions I am frequently asked by new SENCOs is, 'but what is the threshold for SEN?' As ever, SENCOs need to go back to the SEND Code of Practice (DfE and DoH, 2015). Yet, there are other tensions also related to the term and SENCOs leading on inclusive practice need to be aware of these.

One of the criticisms muted is the retention of the term and definition of Special Educational Needs as set out in the 1981 Education Act. The use of the term has been retained despite the recommendation of the Ofsted report (2010), which suggested that the term SEN was used too widely and that it did not represent children accurately; it was too broad. The suggestion from the Ofsted report was that while the term SEN was problematic in its application, the use of additional terms could equally impact on outcomes for the child or young person. They further suggested that categorisation should be moved away from, and a more critical approach was required when using such terms. In practical terms, this means that as a SENCO you need to be clear regarding how the legal definition of SEN is applied in your school.

A further criticism of retaining the term SEN is the impact it can have on the individual. Glazzard (2013) argues that the term SEN is pathological and creates division, thus working against the notion of inclusion and, as a consequence, failing the child. From a practical perspective, this is something a SENCO needs to be mindful of – how does the 'label' SEN potentially create possible exclusion for the pupil? Certainly, Ekins is in agreement and suggests that the continued use of the term is 'complex and ambiguous' (2012, p. 5), which reflects many of the concerns I often hear from SENCOs regarding consistently and accurately applying the term.

However, as Petersen (cited in Williams et al., 2009) argues, the term is enshrined within law, which in turn is cited in a raft of educational policy. To change the terminology, Petersen argues, may create an even more disjointed system and draw away from the key aims of legislation, thereby further denting confidence, particularly in relation to parents, which may present the argument for the continued retention of the term in the new statutory guidance. In short, this is the definition we are working with. It could also be argued that there are greater, more pressing issues to be considering in the realm of SEN, beyond the wording of the legal definition. To overly focus on this issue could prove to be a red herring. Perhaps one of the key issues related to the term is when the label can lead to low expectations (Stobbs, 2014). This therefore places a further responsibility on the SENCO as a leader to ensure that those within their setting are clear regarding what it means to have 'special educational needs', as well as ensuring that expectations are high for all pupils. Later in the book we will consider practical strategies you can adopt to help further your colleagues understanding, in general and specific terms.

Ideas in action

Having considered what SEN and inclusion means to you, you need to explore whether your staff have a similar and/or different understanding.

Staff CPD: SEN and inclusion

It may be helpful to request time for a session where, as a whole staff, you look at the collective understanding of the terms SEN and inclusion. You can also look at what, as a school, you determine to be inclusive practice.

This might take the following format:

- Ensure all staff are invited, including teaching assistants and supervision staff.
- Ask everyone to write down their definition of SEN and what an inclusive school means to them.

- Share with staff the definitions of inclusion.
- Share what the school policies say regarding inclusion. Link to the legal perspective – for example the SEND Code of Practice as the statutory guidance for the 2014 Children and Families Act.
- Ask staff to consider what an inclusive classroom would look like – what is the 'core' offer of the school? This sets the bench mark for expectations regarding quality first teaching in the classrooms.
- Put the staff into groups and ask them to collectively agree a 'core' offer. This will help determine the 'additional to and different from'.
- Ask the teams to present their findings to the rest of the group – encourage debate.
- Share with the group the legal definition of SEN and the graduated approach to identification. Ask them to refer back to their own definition and compare.
- Note issues which have arisen to plan for further training – either individual, group or whole-school.

Setting longer-term, strategic priorities

This chapter has encouraged you to consider the experience of inclusion in your school from an individual and collective level, as well as through the lens of policy and theory. The chapter has also challenged you to think about what inclusion and SEN means to you, as well as the perspective of your colleagues. The process of reflection may be highlighting to you areas which you think would warrant further investigation. As such, you can use your reflections, and those of others, to begin to shape your strategic priorities.

Ideas in action

Given what you have discovered, what do you consider to be the top three priorities to support inclusion in your school?

Rank the priorities in order and look at the first priority.

Ask yourself, what would have to change or be done for you to meet this target? What would look different in your school if this target was achieved?

Detail the specific actions you can take to meet these priorities and group these into the medium- and short-term.

For example, 'Develop staff understanding regarding quality first teaching and inclusive practice' is a long-term, strategic target.

Actions may include:

- Staff CPD relating to 'everyday' quality first inclusive teaching.
- Termly learning walks.
- Mentoring/pairing up of supportive peers.
- SENCO, or another colleague, taking classes (depending on time allocation) to allow colleagues to observe their class and identify potential barriers.

Note, we will look more specifically at creating an action plan in the chapter related to SLT.

In summary

This chapter has explored what it means to be an operational and a strategic leader, however primarily the chapter has explored what, as a SENCO, you are leading on – namely special educational needs provision and inclusive practice. Whilst the next chapter will focus more on how a SENCO can lead, it is imperative that as a new or current SENCO you are clear regarding the ethos you wish to develop regarding inclusion in your school, ensuring that you are reflecting current policy and the rights of the child. Therefore, you hopefully now have an idea of what SEN inclusion means and how this relates to areas you may wish to prioritise, in a strategic sense, in your setting. The next chapter will explore how you can do this, whether or not you are part of the senior leadership team.

References

Ainscow, M. (2007) 'Taking an inclusive turn', *Journal of Research in Special Educational Needs*, 7 (1), pp. 3–7.

Avramidis, E. and Norwich, B. (2016) 'Special educational needs: The state of research: From methodological purism to pluralistic research progress', in Peer, L. and Reid, G. (eds.) *Special educational needs: A guide for inclusive practice.* London: Sage. pp. 28–44.

Bowers, T., Dee, L. and West, M. (1998) 'The code in action: Some school perceptions of its user-friendliness', *Support for Learning*, 13 (3), pp. 99–104.

Centre of Studies for Inclusive Education. (2014) *What is inclusion?* Available at: www.csie.org.uk/inclusion/what.shtml (Accessed 8th March 2015).

Children and Families Act 2014, ch. 6. Available at: www.legislation.gov.uk/ukpga/2014/6/pdfs/ukpga_20140006_en.pdf (Accessed 1st August 2014).

Cowne, E. (2005) *The SENCO handbook: Working within a whole-school approach.* 5th edn. Abingdon, UK: David Fulton.

Curran, H., Moloney, H., Heavey, A. and Boddison, A. (2018) *It's about time: The impact of SENCO workload on the professional and the school.* Available at: www.bathspa.ac.uk/schools/education/research/senco-workload/ (Accessed 3rd January 2019).

Department for Education (DfE). (2014) *National Curriculum in England: framework for key stages 1 to 4.* Available at: www.gov.uk/government/publications/national-curriculum-in-england-framework-for-key-stages-1-to-4/the-national-curriculum-in-england-framework-for-key-stages-1-to-4 (Accessed 4th September 2014).

Department for Education (DfE) and Department of Health (DoH). (2015) *Special educational needs and disability Code of Practice: 0-25 years.* Available at: www.gov.uk/government/uploads/system/uploads/attachment_data/file/398815/SEND_Code_of_Practice_January_2015.pdf (Accessed 1st February 2015).

Department for Education and Skills (DfES). (2001) *Special educational needs Code of Practice.* Available at: webarchive.nationalarchives.gov.uk/20130401151715/www.education.gov.uk/publications/eOrderingDownload/0581-2001-SEN-CodeofPractice.pdf (Accessed 20th September 2014).

Department of Education and Science (DES). (1978) *Special educational needs: Report of the committee of enquiry into the education of handicapped children and young people.* Available at: www.educationengland.org.uk/documents/warnock/warnock1978.html (Accessed 30th September 2014).

Derrington, C. (1997) 'A case for unpacking? Redefining the role of the SENCO in the light of the Code of Practice', *Support for Learning*, 12 (3), pp. 111–115.

The Education (Special Educational Needs Co-ordinators) (England) (Amendment) Regulations 2009 (SI 2009/1387). Available at: http://dera.ioe.ac.uk/10702/5/uksi_20091387_en.pdf (Accessed 14th September 2013).

Education Act 1981, ch. 60. Available at: www.legislation.gov.uk/ukpga/1981/60/pdfs/ukpga_19810060_en.pdf (Accessed 5th July 2016).

Ekins, A. (2012) *The changing face of special educational needs: Impact and implications for SENCos and their schools.* Abingdon, UK: Routledge.

Ellis, S. and Tod, J. (2014) 'Chapter 5. Special educational needs and inclusion: Reflection, renewal and reality', *Journal of Research in Special Educational Needs*, 14 (3), pp. 205–210.

Farrell, M. (2004) *Inclusion at the crossroads: Special education – concepts and values.* London: David Fulton.

Garner, P. (1996) '"Go forth and coordinate!" What special needs coordinators think about the Code of Practice', *School Organisation*, 16 (2), pp. 179–186.

Glazzard, J. (2013) 'A critical interrogation of the contemporary discourses associated with inclusive education in England', *Journal of Research in Special Educational Needs*, 13 (3), pp. 182–188.

Glazzard, J., Stokoe, J., Hughes, A., Netherwood, A. and Neve, L. (2015) *Teaching and supporting children with special educational needs and disabilities in primary schools.* London: Learning Matters.

Griffiths, D. and Dubsky, R. (2012) 'Evaluating the impact of the new National Award for SENCos: Transforming landscapes or gardening in a gale?', *British Journal of Special Education*, 39 (4), pp. 164–172.

Hodkinson, A. (2016) *Key issues in special educational needs and inclusion*. London: Sage.

House of Commons Education and Skills Committee. (2006) *Special educational needs: Third report of the session 2005–06*. (HC 478-1). London: The Stationery Office.

Layton, L. (2005) 'Special educational needs coordinators and leadership: A role too far?', *Support for Learning*, 20 (2), pp. 53–59.

Liasidou, A. (2012) 'Inclusive education and critical pedagogy at the intersections of disability, race, gender and class', *Journal for Critical Education Policy Studies*, 10 (1), pp. 168–184.

Morewood, G. (2012) 'Is the "Inclusive SENCo" still a possibility? A personal perspective', *Support for Learning*, 27 (2), pp. 73–76.

National College of Teaching and Learning. (2014) *National Award for special educational needs co-ordination: Learning outcomes*. Available at: www.gov.uk/government/uploads/system/uploads/attachment_data/file/354172/nasc-learning-outcomes-final.pdf (Accessed 1st September 2014).

Norwich, B. (2014) 'Changing policy and legislation and its effects on inclusive and special education: A perspective from England', *British Journal of Special Education*, 41 (4), p. 40.

Office for Standards in Education (Ofsted). (2010) *The special educational needs and disability review: A statement is not enough*. Available at: www.gov.uk/government/uploads/system/uploads/attachment_data/file/413814/Special_education_needs_and_disability_review.pdf (Accessed 5th October 2015).

Oldham, J. and Radford, J. (2011) 'Secondary SENCo leadership: A universal or specialist role?', *British Journal of Special Education*, 38 (3), pp. 126–134.

Pearson, S. (2008) 'Deafened by silence or by the sound of footsteps? An investigation of the recruitment, induction and retention of special educational needs coordinators (SENCOs) in England', *Journal of Research in Special Educational Needs*, 8 (2), pp. 96–110.

Pearson, S. (2010) 'The role of Special Educational Needs Co-coordinators (SENCOs): "To be or not to be"', *Psychology of Education Review*, 34 (2), pp. 30–38.

Rosen-Webb, S. (2011) 'Nobody tells you how to be a SENCo', *British Journal of Special Education*, 38 (4), pp. 159–168.

Stobbs, P. (2014) 'Chapter 3. Overview of previous national SEND achievements and their fit with current SEND policy directions', *Journal of Research in Special Educational Needs*, 14 (2), pp. 128–132.

Szwed, C. (2007a) 'Reconsidering the role of the primary special educational needs co-ordinator: Policy, practice and future priorities', *British Journal of Special Education*, 34 (2), pp. 96–104.

Szwed, C. (2007b) 'Managing from the middle? Tensions and dilemmas in the role of the primary school special educational needs coordinator', *School Leadership & Management*, 27 (5), pp. 437–451.

Thomas, G. and Loxley, A. (2007) *Deconstructing special education and constructing inclusion*. Maidenhead, UK: Open University Press.

Tissot, C. (2013) 'The role of SENCos as leaders', *British Journal of Special Education*, 40 (1), pp. 33–40.

Warnock, M. (2005) *Special education needs: A new look*. London: Continuum.

Williams, T., Lamb, B., Norwich, B. and Peterson, L. (2009) 'Special educational needs has outlived its usefulness: A debate', *Journal of Research in Special Educational Needs*, 9 (3), pp. 199–217.

The SENCO as a leader

To be or not to be on the senior leadership team

The previous chapter has explored the role of the SENCO as a leader, specifically exploring the nature of the operational and strategic aspects of the role and how these interlink, as well as considering the areas which the SENCO is leading and advocating on –primarily inclusion and special educational needs.

However, whether you are part of the senior leadership team (SLT) or not, the aim is to ensure that there is a strong voice for inclusion and for children with SEN within school, and to ensure the short- and long-term development of effective school-wide practice. Therefore, having considered the overall moral and strategic purpose of inclusion, this chapter will seek to explore leadership in a more practical sense, specifically considering the role of the SLT in relation to the SENCO role, and what the advantages and disadvantages being part of the SLT can bring. The previous 2001 Code stated, 'Many schools find it effective for the SENCO to be a member of the senior leadership team' (DfES, 2001, p. 51). This was also later echoed in the government document, *Removing Barriers to Achievement* (DfES, 2004). The current *SEND Code of Practice* subtly emphasises this point further by stating, 'They [the SENCO] will be most effective in that role if they are part of the school leadership team' (DfE and DoH, 2015, p. 108). Certainly, as the earlier chapter identified, it is not advantageous to separate the operational and strategic aspects of the role, and a direct link could be drawn between *being strategic* and *being a leader*. Therefore, this infers that seniority within the school is required. However, the requirement for the SENCO to be part of the SLT is not a mandatory requirement, and was not adopted as part of the 2008/2009 SENCO regulations and the revised SEND Code of Practice (DfE and DoH, 2015), despite the suggestion of the House of Commons Education and Skills Committee (2006).

Equally, being part of the senior leadership structure is not something all SENCOs aspire to. SENCOs may feel that they do not need, or want, to be part of the SLT to enable them to effectively execute their role. Therefore, this presents an inevitable situation where practice will vary between school settings. As such, this chapter will take into account the varying contexts within which SENCOs work and will consider the SENCO both as part of the SLT, as well as taking a more pragmatic approach through considering whether it is necessary to be part of the SLT to bring about meaningful change, or whether there are other ways in which you can lead on SEN and inclusion in your school, regardless of your position. The chapter will consider the differences between traditional means of leadership, as well as the importance of status. Given that many SENCOs are not part of the SLT, the chapter will specifically consider those who are not part of it, and look at practical ways in which you can develop the status of your role, and of inclusion and SEN, within your school so that you can begin to lead as a SENCO and consider ways in which you can create impact, both at an operational and a strategic level.

In summary this chapter will focus on:

- the role of the SENCO and the SLT;
- I'm not on SLT, but I think I should be;
- the status of the SENCO role;
- leading without being part of SLT; leading with status;
- developing your status as a brand new SENCO;
- developing your status as a more established SENCO; and
- creating priority through a development plan.

The role of the SENCO and the senior leadership team (SLT)

As stated above, the SEND Code of Practice (DfE and DoH, 2015) is clear that the SENCO has an important strategic role, alongside the head teacher and governing body, and that the SENCO will be 'most effective if they are part of the school leadership team' (DfE and DoH, 2015, p. 108). However, the challenge is that being part of the SLT is not mandatory and so the recommendation does not have to be regarded within schools. In a recent survey of SENCOs, over 50% stated that they were part of the SLT due to their SENCO role (Curran et al., 2018). However, a further exploration of the data indicated that of the 1900 plus responses, 62% of primary SENCOs were part of SLT due to their SENCO role, whilst only 22% of secondary SENCOs were in a similar position. This further indicates the variation that SENCOs are experiencing regarding the seniority of their role, illustrating that the context that SENCOs work in may influence whether they are part of the SLT. In addition to this, school structures are school specific. With the relatively recent advancement of free schools and multi-academy trusts (MATs) it could be argued that this has introduced even more diversity. For example, such diversity can be seen in alternative management structures, including 'Directors for Inclusion' who oversee SENCOs in individual schools within a MAT. It is noteworthy that the revised SEND Code of Practice (DfE and DoH, 2015) does not currently address the issue of multi-academy trusts and refers to SENCOs working in individual schools.

Research has typically suggested that for a SENCO to adopt a strong strategic role within the school, in essence to be an effective SENCO, it is crucial for them to be a member of the leadership team (Szwed, 2007; Pearson, 2010; Oldham and Radford, 2011; Tissot, 2013). Szwed's (2007) research found that if the SENCO is a member of the leadership team, then there is a greater chance of the SENCO fulfilling their duties, with the key influencing factor being the enhanced credibility of the role. Mackenzie (2007) agrees, stating that leadership and management are implicit within the position. Tissot (2013) concurs and suggests that if the SENCO is not part of the SLT, then this can stifle the vision of the role as well as the implementation of the role in practice, a view supported by Qureshi (2014). It is certainly interesting to consider whether a SENCO being part of the SLT is a reflection on the school's position and priority regarding inclusion.

However, Layton's (2005) research with SENCOs developed this idea further. The findings from her research suggested that not only did SENCOs themselves think that membership to the SLT was imperative, but also that non-membership was the greatest barrier to achieving the moral purpose of the role. When we consider the previous chapter, which explored the idea of creating cultural change, Oldham and Radford (2011) argue that formal managerial status, through SLT membership, would give the SENCO more influence within the school and, as a consequence, raise the profile of children with SEN. They further argue that leadership is highly relevant to the role.

This is not to suggest that membership on the leadership team is automatically viewed in a positive light. Pearson (2008) suggests that SENCOs can become marginalised when part of the SLT. Equally, to have a SLT without a SENCO can mean that inclusion and SEN are then the responsibility of all on the team, rather than the remit of one person. There are also practical issues. Some SENCOs in Pearson's research stated that they were 'content not to have the additional responsibilities associated with being a member of the management team' (2008, p. 104). Given the research regarding SENCO workload, it is understandable that SENCOs may not wish to extend their role (Curran et al., 2018). In addition to this, SENCOs may often feel that it is beneficial to remain in the classroom, teaching, as it keeps them rooted to good practice, as well as providing them with the opportunity to model good practice for colleagues.

Something to think about

If you are part of SLT, why are you part of SLT? Is this due to your SENCO role, or due to another role you hold?

When you are in SLT meetings, what 'hat' are you wearing? How do you ensure that the priority of inclusion permeates all aspects of your endeavours? Do you find yourself asking the team, 'Yes, but what about ...?'

Below provides some initial thoughts regarding the advantages to being part of the SLT, but also some considerations. What do you consider to be the pros and cons for a SENCO as part of the SLT?

The SENCO on the SLT

Advantages:

The voice of the SENCO can permeate all discussions, both operational and strategic, at a senior level.
SEN can be advocated for across all levels and can become an intrinsic consideration for all aspects of decision making.
The SENCO will have a wider awareness of school priorities and how these link to SEN.
Due to SLT 'status' the SENCO may be viewed as having the necessary authority to affect change in their setting.
Issues related to inclusion and SEN can be quickly and easily communicated to the SLT.

Considerations:

If the SENCO is part of SLT:

The SENCO on the SLT can lead to a separatist approach, i.e. the SENCO is then wholly responsible for SEN in the school. As such this can lead to an isolated approach.
Being part of the SLT can lead to an expansion of the SENCO role. This can create additional time pressures on the SENCO.
SLT activities can draw attention away from SENCO activities.

If the SENCO is not part of the SLT:

The SENCO may lack influence when sharing identified priorities, decision making etc.
The SENCO may be seen as lacking in the status required to affect change; the SENCO may be ignored.

I'm not on SLT, but I think I should be

For some of you, as stated above, you may be breathing a sigh of relief that you are not part of the SLT with the challenges that this can bring. You may feel that you already have the necessary support and status within school; perhaps this is echoed through the overarching school ethos. As such you may feel that you have the tools to effectively execute your role without being a member of the SLT. On the other hand, you may feel that your role, and the school, would be better served if you were part of this team.

For example, you may be:

- a few years into the SENCO role and now feel confident to begin to focus on more strategic elements;
- looking to develop and extend your skills, with a view to moving into senior leadership;
- seeking to ensure that SEN and inclusion is meaningfully integrated as part of the school development plan and believe that you need to be part of the SLT to facilitate this;
- feeling that there needs to be a greater focus, at a senior level, on issues related to SEN and inclusion; and
- feeling that there needs to be an increased status attached to your role for you to create meaningful change.

So, what can you do?

- Decide what you want.
- Take soundings.
- State your case.

In terms of deciding what you want, this relates to whether you want to make changes to your contract, your role or whether you want access to SLT meetings as and when you think it is necessary. It would then be useful to take soundings, perhaps with your SEN governor and/or another senior leader, before you state your case to the head teacher. Consider how you see this working. This is where the earlier chapter, which suggests sharing with the SLT and the governing body the extent of your role, is so important. Not only do the 2008/2009 SENCO regulations state that it is the responsibility of the governing body to determine the leadership and management role of the SENCO, but it is essential to remind *everybody* that the responsibility of SEN provision and inclusive practice is not the remit of the SENCO, but the responsibility of the school leaders. This includes the following from the SEND Code of Practice:

- Teachers are responsible and accountable for the progress and development of the pupils in their class, including where pupils access support from teaching assistants or specialist staff (DfE and DoH, 2015, p. 99).
- The school should ensure that the SENCO has sufficient time and resources to carry out these functions. This should include providing the SENCO with sufficient administrative support and time away from teaching to enable them to fulfil their responsibilities in a similar way to other important strategic roles within a school (DfE and DoH, 2015, p. 109).

It would then be useful to arrange a time to meet with either your line manager or your head teacher to discuss your view. You may want to think about timelines and the additional skills you will not only bring, but would also need support in developing, as part of the SLT.

Oldham and Radford (2011) argue that while it is preferable for the SENCO to be part of the SLT, the question is redundant as both require leadership, perhaps suggesting that there is a difference between being a formal leader and demonstrating leadership. Therefore, focusing overly on whether the SENCO is part of the SLT may be misplaced. In a sense it may sound as if we are talking about joining a secret club, which holds all the answers, and this is not necessarily the case. It could be argued that instead the focus should be on whether the SENCO has the necessary status to effectively undertake their role, including the status and support required to create meaningful change at both an operational and strategic level across the school.

The status of the SENCO role

If we were to review and condense the literature detailed above, the five reasons why the SENCO should be part of the SLT are:

- it gives credibility to the role;
- it helps to shape and determine the shared vision for inclusion and SEN in the school;
- it helps support the implementation of processes and change;
- it helps enact the moral purpose of the role; and
- it provides influence across other areas of the school, as well as the SENCO role.

However, leading as a SENCO is not simply going to be facilitated by being part of the SLT. Leadership can equally be about having the perceived status to effect change in your setting. It could also be argued that the five reasons above can also be facilitated by ensuring that SEN is embedded across the school, through SENCO actions, but equally that the role is held in high esteem by school staff, including senior leaders. Certainly, research I have undertaken, which support the view of Griffiths and Dubsky (2012), suggests that SENCOs do not perceive a lack of SLT membership as an impenetrable barrier to try to affect change and influence wider school policy.

Tissot (2013) would suggest that leadership is central to affecting cultural change. This, therefore, implies that the status of the SENCO role is imperative to ensure its effectiveness. However, Pearson (2008) suggests that the role of the SENCO is typically not in a senior position and, as a consequence, the role itself can be ineffective at influencing whole-school policy. It could equally be argued that the lack of status stems from its definition, which has partly focused on the specialist, rather than managerial, nature of the role (Imants et al., 2001 cited in Szwed, 2007). While Mackenzie (2007) suggests that a specialist role can bring status, the issue is that this can mean that the area of SEN is then viewed as specialist, and as a consequence, the remit of supporting children with SEN is not within the responsibilities or capabilities of the class teacher (Hodkinson, 2016). There are clear implications for the SENCO here. SENCOs need to be clear on the remit of their role, what the parameters are and what they should be doing, as well as the responsibilities of others. As stated in the earlier chapter, the SENCO needs to ensure that their role, and the roles of others, are clearly defined, and those they work with understand these definitions. This cannot be overstated and is one aspect where the SENCO can take control.

Rosen-Webb (2011), in agreement with Szwed (2007), suggests that a lack of status for the SENCO has created barriers and has therefore impacted on the effectiveness of the position. It could be argued that the perceived status of the SENCO role has been an issue since its inception (Lewis et al., 1995, cited in Derrington, 1997) and, in part, this has been linked to training and qualifications. In 1998, the National Teaching Standards stipulated that while there was a need for teachers to have specific experience and training regarding SEN (Cowne, 2005), this was not a requirement. Training and qualifications have been offered, although not universally. For example, the SENCO standards suggested that the person undertaking the role should be educated to be degree level. However, the need for qualified teacher status (QTS) was not stipulated until 2008, resulting in some SENCOs not being qualified teachers (Pearson, 2008). During this time, there was some SENCO-specific training, for example Birmingham University offered a postgraduate qualification based on the Teacher Training Agency (TTA) standards (Layton, 2005), but this was optional.

Regarding mandatory qualifications, the most significant shift in legislation was the adoption of the SENCO regulations which came into force in 2009. The 2008 SENCO regulations stated that the person undertaking the role must be a qualified teacher, working at the school, and must have completed the induction period for new teachers. The later amended 2009 SENCO regulations further stated that SENCOs new to the post from 1st September 2009 had to achieve the National Award for Special Educational Needs Coordination (NA SENCO) (Robertson, 2012). This illustrated a dramatic shift regarding the level of qualifications required for the role, where historically it may have been undertaken by a learning support assistant (LSA) under the supervision of the SLT (Cowne, 2005; Pearson, 2008). While the requirement to be a qualified teacher was significant, it was the introduction of the NA SENCO through the 2009 SENCO regulations that raised the profile and significance of the role (Rosen-Webb, 2011; Robertson, 2012). It was the dual focus at a national and local policy level that had crucially had an impact (Robertson, 2012).

Something to think about

If you are doing, or have done, the NA SENCO, who knows what you are doing/have done? Have you told your SEN governor about it? Do staff know? This is something to shout about – it is a Masters level qualification!

Given the changes brought in with the 2008, and later amended 2009, SENCO regulations, it is notable that there remain issues relating to status, despite wider recognition of the role (Qureshi, 2014). Interestingly, Mackenzie (2007) highlights that parents viewed the SENCO position as more high status, as they would typically go to the SENCO for advice relating to resources, contacts or general knowledge regarding SEN. We will look at the process for referral and access to the SENCO later in the book. However, such interpretations further indicate the tensions between the specialist and strategic role (Mackenzie, 2007; Rosen-Webb, 2011; Qureshi, 2014). In contrast to this view, research by Layton (2005) suggests that the SENCOs did not consider that their role was viewed as a leadership role and, consequently, they wanted higher status. Interestingly, it was Layton who suggested that SENCO training should be mandatory.

However, Pearson (2010) argues that the SENCO can only be truly effective if SEN becomes a whole-school issue, stating that there needs to be a shared philosophical position; reflective of the notion of inclusive education as stipulated by Humphrey and Lewis (2008). This further highlights the importance, as discussed in the earlier chapter, of ensuring that as a SENCO you lead on, and develop, the school understanding and ethos to special educational needs and inclusion. This develops the argument beyond that of status and is not a one-off staff meeting. It is an on-going, longer term piece of work. Pearson goes on to argue that the SENCO needs to be embedded within the school leadership structure to facilitate this, echoing previous work (Cowne, 2005; Szwed, 2007). The SENCO needs to focus on developing and embracing strategic opportunities as they will not necessarily present themselves. This, therefore, is the focus of the next section.

Leading without being part of SLT: leading with status

This next section takes the view that there are a number of ways, as a SENCO, in which you can lead on SEN, with or without the traditional notion of SLT status. These are tried and tested tips from either my own experience of being a SENCO, or from SENCOs I have the privilege to work with, all of which have the primary aim of keeping SEN and inclusion front and centre in terms of school activities. It is also noteworthy that perhaps a causal link is being made here, between raising the status of the SENCO within school, and increasing the prominence and visibility of SEN and inclusion across the school, which, in turn, will increase the potential status and importance of SEN and inclusion in general. This section has been divided into three parts: activities which may be more pertinent to brand new SENCOs, those which may be relevant to SENCOs who have some experience, and how to develop a strategic plan for SEN.

Developing your status as a brand new SENCO

Policy is your friend

The 2014 Children and Families Act and the SEND Code of Practice (DfE and DoH, 2015) is the starting point. To lead effectively in your setting, it is imperative to ensure that you are familiar with current legislation. Not only do you need to ensure that you are following statutory processes, but equally you can use policy to further specific aims and priorities within your setting. For example:

- My PhD research looked at the implementation of the SEND reforms from the perspective of the SENCO. SENCOs who did not have typical notions of authority, basically who weren't part of the SLT, saw the introduction of the SEND Code of Practice (DfE and DoH, 2015) as a means through which they could further specific agendas in school. Essentially, they could refer to the new guidance as the vehicle for promoting change in their settings. For example, the principles of the SEND Code of Practice are centred around working with pupils and families. For many SENCOs, at the time, this enabled them to shift the focus within schools towards reviewing and developing parental participation because the SEND Code of Practice has such a strong focus on this element. Consider if you can use the principles of the SEND Code of Practice to help you identify priorities in your school.

- It is also important to ensure that senior leaders and the governing body are aware of the policy, and their role within this. Some school leaders, including the governing body, may not be aware of their statutory responsibilities. This is something you can share with them.

Ensure your role is understood

One of the key aspects to developing the status of your role is ensuring that those around you have clarity regarding your role. It is interesting to note that the National SENCO Workload Survey suggested that SENCOs did not feel that their role was understood particularly well, with 46% of all respondents stating that they felt senior managers understood their role, but only 27% believing that other colleagues understood their role (Curran et al., 2018). Therefore, the following are suggestions which might help those around you develop their understanding of the SENCO role.

- Consider arranging a regular weekly, fortnightly or monthly meeting with your head teacher. These sessions can be used to make them aware of any key issues related to SEN provision in your school. However, this session can also be used to share with them your plans and priorities for the strategic development of SEN provision in your school, as well as making them aware of any potential barriers or challenges that you are experiencing. If you can't do this with your head teacher, then arrange this with your line manager or other senior leaders and request that time is set aside in leadership meetings for this information to be passed on.
- Meet with your SEN governor to ensure that they understand not only your role, but the difference between your operational and strategic aims/responsibilities.
- Ensure that those around you are aware that you are completing the NA SENCO – this is a Masters level qualification. Ensure that both your senior leadership team and your SEN governor understand what this entails. Share the learning outcomes which relate to leadership with your SLT. During reviews with your line manager, review the learning outcomes and discuss how you will meet these.
- Share the assignment/s you have written for the NA SENCO with your senior leadership team and/or SEN governor. This can be a good way of not only highlighting the requirements of the NA SENCO, but also can be a development opportunity for your member of staff or SEN governor, through reading your work on a specific subject. For example, if you focused your assignment on the SENCO role, this could be a great opportunity to also highlight your role to others. You can ask them to proof read at the same time!

- Use the earlier chapters to be clear on the parameters of your role. Establish roles and responsibilities and how these translate into your school. Consider how you share these with you colleagues. A good starting place is the SEN policy, but you may need to consider other ways in which you can do this to ensure the message is embedded. Chapter 5, 'Leading and supporting colleagues', explores this further.

Developing your status as a more established SENCO

Get in on the act

A primary tension related to whether or not the SENCO is a part of the SLT is whether or not the SENCO has the required status and authority to effect change in their setting. This can mean that you need to create opportunities to be strategic in your setting. Part of this relates to 'knowledge-transfer' between you and the SLT, and vice versa. How are messages and decisions communicated between parties? In addition to this, two way communication means that you can ensure that you are able to advocate for SEN and inclusion. If you are not part of the SLT you might want to consider if there are times of the year, or specific meetings, which you think you must attend to enable you to develop communication between you and the SLT. Determine which meetings you think would be useful to attend in school and why. For example:

- There may be occasions where you attend specific SLT meetings. Discuss with the head teacher the planned meetings and focus for the term and agree with them which of these you think it would be useful for you to attend.
- Pupil progress meetings. Do you attend pupil progress meetings? Consider whether you think you should attend these meetings. It can be very useful, particularly in terms of early identification of need. If you do not attend, you need to think about how information will be shared with you from these meetings, and the processes which will subsequently occur.
- Consider your role in parent evenings. Are you part of the 'booking' system for parents – can they opt to see you in this period? Consider how your role as SENCO can be facilitated and seen as part of these meetings. This will enable you to not only develop links with parents, but will also increase the visibility of your role in school.

> **Ideas in action**
>
> James has been a primary SENCO for four years. He has completed the NA SENCO and has two days per week to focus on the role. The development

of SEN and inclusive practice is a priority for the school. Yet James is not currently part of the SLT. James took the following actions:

- He met with the head teacher to share his SEND development plan. He also shared this with his SEN governor.
- He outlined to the head teacher and SEN governor the importance of ensuring SEN and inclusive practice is part of the wider, whole-school agenda (refer to Chapter 3, 'The SENCO as a leader: your role, your school, your ethos'). They related this to the school's overarching aims.
- He shared with them the NA SENCO learning outcomes related to leadership.
- He identified the meetings he needed to be part of, specifically pupil progress meetings.
- He requested that he should be invited to specific SLT meetings. He and his head teacher identified instances in the year when this would occur.
- He focused his NA SENCO assignment on the leadership aspect of the SENCO role and shared this with his head teacher and SEN governor.

Grow your team of advocates

The 2014 Children and Families Act states that there is a duty within mainstream schools in England to ensure there is a designated member of staff at the school who is responsible for SEN provision. It does not state that the SENCO should have a team or administrative support, although the SEND Code of Practice does state that the SENCO should have 'sufficient administrative support ... to enable them to fulfil their responsibilities in a similar way to other important strategic roles within a school' (2015, p. 109). As such, this means that the SENCO needs to consider how to grow their teams, either formally or informally. Later in the book we will look at the importance of growing your team in order to support the facilitation of the role as part of meeting the challenges associated with it. However, having a team can be equally important when considering how to lead on SEN in your school.

- You need SEN advocates at every level – be explicit about this. If you are not currently part of the SLT, who is 'the voice' for SEN and inclusion at every senior leadership team meeting if you are not there?
- Create an open channel of communication. For example, is there a designated member of the SLT who is your 'go to'? They can ensure that they raise key issues with the SLT on your behalf.

- Ensure that you use time with your SEN governor to raise key issues, and state which of these you need to be highlighted at the next governing body meeting. For example, ask them to ensure that they consider SEN and inclusion when they review existing and new policies. If you are part of a multi-academy trust, what is your route to ensuring that those who need to know about specific issues, do?

- Consider the other meetings which take place at school. If you work within a large primary or a secondary school, it would be impossible to attend every phase or departmental meeting. As such, who is going to be the SEN advocate in these meetings? Can you approach a colleague and ask them to ensure that issues related to SEN and inclusion are raised or queried as and when necessary? Immediately, you will then begin to grow your team of SEN and inclusion advocates across the school.

- It is a classic parenting issue that you can be stating something yourself, until you are blue in the face, but when Granny says the same thing, the kids listen. It is infuriating, but true. The same can be said of education. I have heard the frustrations of SENCOs who do not feel heard when they are trying to relay specific messages, only for someone 'external' to come in, say the same thing, and get a response. This is something that you might have to, not necessarily accept, but use to your advantage. Growing your own team of advocates outside of school, for example through networking on the NA SENCO, through SENCO clusters, or via online networks, can be a useful way of highlighting what works in other schools and which might also be advantageous to try in your school. This can be a quick way of getting colleagues on board, as these will be 'tired and tested' ideas.

Be a 'covert' entrepreneur

It could be considered that not all strategic leadership is overt. This is potentially an important consideration when we look at the rate of changes, and related requirements, which teachers are dealing with every day. This can make leadership challenging. How do you motivate colleagues to engage with new initiatives when they are already weary? How can you add to their workload when you know they are already under significant amounts of pressure? As such you need to think about more covert ways. Consider how you can overtly and covertly strengthen the message of inclusion within your school. The equivalent of hiding the veggies in the spaghetti bolognaise. The next chapter will explore more explicitly the ways in which you can lead and support colleagues, however you might also want to consider the following:

- Permeating your environment with your expectations. For example, a SENCO I worked with used to put on every piece of school paperwork 'Every teacher is a teacher of SEND'.

53

- Reviewing the language used in school and considering how it fits with your ethos regarding SEN and inclusion, as discussed in the previous chapter. For example, when considering the policies in your school, is the language person first, i.e. children with special educational needs or additional educational needs, rather than SEN children?
- What information is available around the school which pertains to SEN? Are there references to inclusion on your school newsletter, for example? How much is SEN and inclusion part of the everyday narrative at school. Consider whether information related to SEN, in general and more specifically, is easily accessible for teachers.

Creating priority through a development plan

Make sure SEN and inclusion is a priority – make it part of the plan

As stated in Chapter 3, 'The SENCO as a leader: your role, your school, your ethos', a key part to leading both operationally and strategically is ensuring that you are clear as to the areas you are leading on, and your priorities for these areas. In the previous chapter you were challenged to identify three priorities for the development of SEN and inclusive practice in your school and then to think about what would need to change for these targets to be met. A SEN development plan can be an important tool to not only ensure that SEN is considered in a strategic sense, through the creation of strategic opportunities (as earlier discussed), but also in creating a plan to which you as a SENCO, and others, can work with to enable you to move beyond 'firefighting'. Therefore, consider the following:

- What do staff know about the current situation regarding SEN in your school? Do they know the percentage of children with an Education, Health and Care (EHC) plan or at SEN support, and how, as a school, you compare to the national average? It may be useful to know where your school stands in relation to the national picture. This can also be used as a tool to help you determine priorities for your SEN development plan. Sharing of the wider picture with staff will also help them see the relevance of your plan.
- Think about how you can communicate this to staff. This could be through a SEN newsletter, a noticeboard or a standing item at the start of every staff meeting.
- Develop a clear and cohesive SEN development plan. What are the priorities, both long and short term, for SEN and inclusion in your school? How does this relate to your vision, as discussed in the earlier chapter, for SEN and inclusion in your school. This needs to relate to the overarching aims of the school, further highlighting the importance of communication with your SLT.

- Make sure you are aware of wider school priorities and how the identified SEN priorities inter-link. Be explicit on your plan regarding wider links.
- Ensure that you share your intended priorities with your colleagues, senior leaders and SEN governor. Ask for comment, as they may have identified different priorities. It is imperative, as a SENCO, to ensure that you do not become isolated. Asking for comment or review can help you look towards your colleagues for support.
- Once you have identified your priorities, and shared this with the SLT, consider other stakeholders who should be informed and involved with the shaping of the plan. Have you shared the school priorities for inclusion and SEN with pupils and parents? Later in the book we explore developing effective relationships with pupils and parents, however, ensuring that they are part of developing the whole-school plan towards developing inclusion is important. You could ask a small group of parents to come in and comment on your ideas. They may have very different priorities!
- Share your ideas within your wider network of SENCOs. Liaise with other SENCOs as to the actions you have identified and ask for their feedback. Seek their guidance to help you identify key actions and ask them to share what they are focusing on.
- Use your network of SENCOs to explore how they do things. If they have successfully undertaken one of the areas you have identified as an objective, arrange a time to meet to review what they did.
- Ensure your development plan is broken down into manageable steps, with clear success criteria and designated leads; do not put 'SENCO' down for every single action.
- Look at the actions which you, and others, will need to take to meet these objectives. What would change in your setting for you to know how these objectives have been met? How long, realistically, will it take to meet these aims? Ensure each priority is allocated a time-scale for completion.
- Make sure you share the SEN development plan with the senior leadership team and not only the SEN governor, but also the governing body.
- Share your development plan with parents and children. Consider how you share this information and ensure it is accessible. Consider holding a meeting for parents so you can share how you intend to move forward in your school and further the vision you have determined. Share with parents their potential role within this, but equally invite comments on how they see how things can be developed.

In summary

Essentially, it is unequivocal that being part of the SLT will afford the SENCO opportunities to ensure that SEN and inclusion is embedded within the school. As this chapter has highlighted, the SEND Code of Practice (DfE and DoH, 2015) is clear that the SENCO has an important strategic role, alongside the head teacher and governing body, and that the SENCO will be 'most effective if they are part of the school leadership team' (DfE and DoH, 2015, p. 108). Yet, we know that only approximately half of SENCOs are part of the SLT as part of their SENCO role (Curran et al., 2018). On the other hand, we also know that being part of the SLT will not automatically make you a strategic leader, or indeed give you the necessary authority to effect strategic change in your setting. As a SENCO, whatever your position, in order to lead effectively you need to seek out the opportunities to be strategic, both overt and covert, to ensure that the inclusive ethos you wish to develop permeates your school.

Ideas in action

From the list above, pick out two or three practical activities you can focus on to develop the status of your role in school. For example, create a bulletin which shares with your colleagues the current picture of SEN in your school, including the number of children at SEN support, number of EHC plans, planned training and activities, and your identified priorities for the coming term. Monitor staff response to this. Has this raised their awareness of SEN in general?

References

Children and Families Act 2014, ch. 6. Available at: www.legislation.gov.uk/ukpga/2014/6/pdfs/ukpga_20140006_en.pdf (Accessed 1st August 2014).

Cowne, E. (2005) *The SENCO handbook: Working within a whole-school approach.* 5th edn. Abingdon, UK: David Fulton.

Curran, H., Moloney, H., Heavey, A. and Boddison, A. (2018) *It's about time: The impact of SENCO workload on the professional and the school.* Available at: www.bathspa.ac.uk/schools/education/research/senco-workload/ (Accessed 3rd January 2019).

Department for Education (DfE) and Department of Health (DoH). (2015) *Special educational needs and disability Code of Practice: 0–25 years.* Available at: www.gov.uk/government/uploads/system/uploads/attachment_data/file/398815/SEND_Code_of_Practice_January_2015.pdf (Accessed 1st February 2015).

Department for Education and Skills (DfES). (2001) *Special educational needs Code of Practice.* Available at: webarchive.nationalarchives.gov.uk/20130401151715/www.education.gov.uk/publi

cations/eOrderingDownload/0581-2001-SEN-CodeofPractice.pdf (Accessed 20th September 2014).

Department for Education and Skills (DfES). (2004) *Removing barriers to achievement: The government's strategy for special educational needs*. Available at: webarchive.nationalarchives. gov.uk/20130401151715/www.education.gov.uk/publications/standard/publicationDetail/Page1/ DfES%200117%202004 (Accessed 1st July 2016).

Derrington, C. (1997) 'A case for unpacking? Redefining the role of the SENCO in the light of the Code of Practice', *Support for Learning*, 12 (3), pp. 111–115.

The Education (Special Educational Needs Co-ordinators) (England) (Amendment) Regulations 2009 (SI 2009/1387). Available at: http://dera.ioe.ac.uk/10702/5/uksi_20091387_en.pdf (Accessed 14th September 2013).

The Education (Special Educational Needs Co-ordinators) (England) Regulations 2008 (SI 2008/ 2945). Available at: http://dera.ioe.ac.uk/10702/4/SI%202008%201945.pdf (Accessed 14th September 2013).

Griffiths, D. and Dubsky, R. (2012) 'Evaluating the impact of the new National Award for SENCos: Transforming landscapes or gardening in a gale?', *British Journal of Special Education*, 39 (4), pp. 164–172.

Hodkinson, A. (2016) *Key issues in special educational needs and inclusion*. London: Sage.

House of Commons Education and Skills Committee. (2006) *Special educational needs: Third report of the session* 2005–06. (HC 478-1). London: The Stationery Office.

Humphrey, N. and Lewis, S. (2008) 'What does "inclusion" mean for pupils on the autistic spectrum in mainstream secondary schools?', *Journal of Research in Special Educational Needs*, 8 (3), pp. 132–140.

Layton, L. (2005) 'Special educational needs coordinators and leadership: A role too far?', *Support for Learning*, 20 (2), pp. 53–59.

Mackenzie, S. (2007) 'A review of recent developments in the role of the SENCo in the UK', *British Journal of Special Education*, 34 (4), pp. 212–218.

Oldham, J. and Radford, J. (2011) 'Secondary SENCo leadership: A universal or specialist role?', *British Journal of Special Education*, 38 (3), pp. 126–134.

Pearson, S. (2008) 'Deafened by silence or by the sound of footsteps? An investigation of the recruitment, induction and retention of special educational needs coordinators (SENCOs) in England', *Journal of Research in Special Educational Needs*, 8 (2), pp. 96–110.

Pearson, S. (2010) 'The role of Special Educational Needs Co-coordinators (SENCOs): "To be or not to be"', *Psychology of Education Review*, 34 (2), pp. 30–38.

Qureshi, S. (2014) 'Herding cats or getting heard: The SENCo-teacher dynamic and its impact on teachers' classroom practice', *Support for Learning*, 29 (3), pp. 217–229.

Robertson, C. (2012) 'Special educational needs and disability co-ordination in a changing policy landscape: Making sense of policy from a SENCo's perspective', *Support for Learning*, 27 (2), pp. 77–83.

Rosen-Webb, S. (2011) 'Nobody tells you how to be a SENCo', *British Journal of Special Education*, 38 (4), pp. 159–168.

Szwed, C. (2007) 'Managing from the middle? Tensions and dilemmas in the role of the primary school special educational needs coordinator', *School Leadership & Management*, 27 (5), pp. 437–451.

Tissot, C. (2013) 'The role of SENCos as leaders', *British Journal of Special Education*, 40 (1), pp. 33–40.

Leading and supporting colleagues

Introduction

A key part of the SENCO role is working with colleagues to facilitate effective SEN provision across your setting. This is explicit through the term 'Special Educational Needs *Coordinator*' as opposed to 'Special Educational Needs *Teacher*'. This is, of course, simplifying the role. However, it is imperative for a SENCO to focus on leading and supporting colleagues, as it is neither desirable, or sustainable, for a SENCO to be the person within the school who is solely responsible for identifying and facilitating support for children with additional needs; indeed the SEND Code of Practice (DfE and DoH, 2015) is explicit regarding the central role the teacher should play. As such a key part of the role is to ensure that colleagues are supported in the development of their inclusive practice.

Since the introduction of the most recent SEND Code of Practice (DfE and DoH, 2015) there has been a move towards emphasising the collective responsibility of all teachers, with the SEND Code of Practice stating that all class/subject teachers have responsibility for all children in their class, including those with SEN. This not only underlines the importance of supporting and leading colleagues, but also the importance of ensuring that teachers are aware of their responsibilities. Clarity of roles can help support the development of a collective sense of responsibility, through a clear understanding of each other's roles in school and how these are enacted, including that of the SENCO as explored in the first chapter. In addition to this, it is through leading, supporting and challenging colleagues that a school can continue to develop and improve not only provision for children with SEN, but provision for all children.

This chapter seeks to build on the earlier chapters related to leadership, through a more practical lens. With clarity regarding your role, and the role of others, as well as having a clear view on how you wish the inclusive ethos in your school to develop, this chapter explores the various activities you can undertake to achieve this. The chapter will consider how, in your role as SENCO, you can offer professional support and guidance to ensure the day-to-day operation of the SEN policy, as well as consideration of the strategic development of inclusive practice in your school. The chapter will look at the activities you can undertake at a whole-school level, both short and long term, as well as ways in which you can support individuals and specific groups within your setting who may benefit from more tailored support, for example support staff, newly qualified teachers and teachers who are new to your school.

In summary this chapter will focus on:

- the SENCO role: leading and supporting colleagues;
- unpicking the role of teachers;
- leading and supporting colleagues: a whole-school approach; and
- leading and supporting specific groups.

The SENCO role: leading and supporting colleagues

As with earlier chapters, it is important to return to the SEND Code of Practice (DfE and DoH, 2015) to establish not only the role of the SENCO, but also the role of colleagues, to ensure that parameters are clear. This also ensures that through shared expectations, support and challenge can be offered appropriately. However, perhaps one of the challenges particularly new SENCOs may experience, is that the distribution of magic wands and an increased knowledge of SEN legislation do not automatically occur as soon as you take on the role! It could be argued that perhaps this issue has been compounded because the role of the SENCO continues to be referred to in a singular sense (DfE and DoH, 2015), not only in national policy, but often in school policy too. Certainly, this can be quite daunting for new SENCOs, as you may find that immediately colleagues are asking for support and advice, perhaps in areas or processes which are unfamiliar to you. Later in this chapter we will look at ways in which you can support colleagues with queries, whilst also creating systems and processes to ensure consistency, as well as endeavouring to protect your time. However, it is imperative that new SENCOs, in particular, remember that it is impossible to know everything; you are a coordinator, not a 'do-er', and the phrase, 'I'll get back to you on that' is a requirement!

The theme of the SENCO supporting colleagues permeates the SEND Code of Practice (DfE and DoH, 2015). For SENCOs working in schools, you will be particularly concerned with Chapter 6 of the SEND Code of Practice (DfE and DoH, 2015), as it is this chapter which concerns provision in schools. In terms of the SENCO role and the role of supporting colleagues, the SEND Code of Practice is clear and states, 'The SENCO provides professional guidance to colleagues and will work closely with staff, parents and other agencies (DfE and DoH, 2015, p. 108).

Chapter 6 goes on to state that the SENCO has responsibility for the 'coordination of specific provision made to support individual pupils' with SEN, including those who have EHC plans' (DfE and DoH, 2015, p. 108), which infers that there needs to be effective communication between the SENCO and teacher to ensure that the provision is in place. The chapter further outlines how the SENCO will support teachers through adopting an advisory role in relation to the graduated approach, specifically the Assess, Plan, Do, Review process, as well as reviewing teachers' knowledge and understanding of SEN and related strategies, with specific consideration of how this may need improving. This infers that the SENCO should be aware of their staff training needs and the requirement for continuing professional development (CPD) in their setting. The SEND Code of Practice also describes how the SENCO should be able to 'ensure that pupils with SEN receive appropriate support and high quality teaching' (DfE and DoH, 2015, p. 108), again suggesting that the leadership and support of colleagues is essential.

Knowing your role in relation to the role of your colleague's links directly with understanding how you see SEN provision and inclusion developing in your school, with Cole (2005) suggesting that SENCOs are directly involved in the deliverance of an inclusive agenda. In one sense this means that the SENCO role is not just about providing support, whether this be in an individual or collective sense, but also that SENCOs are tasked with the role of providing challenge, or as Kearns suggests, SENCOs should be questioning 'all forms of exclusive practice' (2005, p. 143). Therefore, as a SENCO, you may find yourself in the position of questioning, or indeed challenging, specific approaches. Later in the book the idea of advocacy for pupils and parents will be explored, however it is vital to consider that leading colleagues does also mean, at times, challenging them through supportive discussions and debate, or through processes which you have devised.

Something to think about

Think about a recent time when you have had to speak to a colleague regarding the provision you expected to be in place for a child or young person. Think about how the conversation developed. Consider the following:

- How did you broach the subject with the colleague?
- How did you ensure that your colleague felt supported, and not threatened?
- What factors helped the discussion?
- What factors inhibited the discussion?
- What could you do differently next time?

It might be useful for new SENCOs to make links with more experienced SENCOs to find out how they manage difficult conversations with colleagues and to explore what has worked for them.

However, prior to exploring how colleagues can be supported in a practical sense, it is imperative to understand the specific, important role of the teacher and what the expectations are in relation to children with additional needs.

Unpicking the role of teachers

In terms of the class/subject teacher role, the SEND Code of Practice (DfE and DoH, 2015) states that it is the teacher's responsibility, with the support of senior leaders, to ensure that regular assessments of pupils' progress are made and should be used to identify any pupils who are making less than expected progress; it should be noted that progress does not solely refer to academic progress, but also refers to, 'where a pupil needs to make additional progress with wider development or social needs in order to make a successful transition to adult life' (DfE and DoH, 2015, p. 95). The SEND Code of Practice goes on to state that the first response to any identified concerns is 'high quality teaching' (2015, p. 95) and, if progress is not as expected, the teacher, with the support of the SENCO, can then determine if there is an underlying SEN which may impact on progress. This highlights the importance, discussed earlier in the book, of developing a shared understanding of what *high quality teaching* looks like in your school. However, perhaps the most important statement within the SEND Code of Practice is that 'Teachers are responsible and accountable for the progress and development of the pupils in their class, including where pupils access support from teaching assistants or specialist staff' (DfE and DoH, 2015, p. 99).

This statement is important for many reasons: it further underlines the 'coordinating' role of the SENCO, but equally highlights the importance of the teacher retaining overall responsibility for all children in their class.

The Deployment and Impact of Support Staff Project (DISS) (Blatchford et al., 2009) was a landmark study which explored the role and deployment of support staff. Over the five year research period, there was an increase in the number of support staff (full-time equivalent) working in schools. The data suggested that one of the key reasons for this rise in support staff was the increase in the number of children with special educational needs in schools, with a significant proportion of support staff deployed to work with children with SEN. Whilst the project found that support staff had a positive impact on teachers, for example positively impacting on workload and stress, the impact on children was less positive, with the report stating, 'the more support pupils received, the less progress they made' (2009, p. 2). It went on to state that the key issue was *how* support staff were deployed, as well as how the staff received support regarding preparedness for their work. This again highlights the importance of the teacher retaining overall responsibility for all pupils, ensuring that they work closely with support staff in the development and facilitation of individual and group intervention.

In relation to the class/subject teacher retaining overall responsibility for their pupils, it is perhaps interesting to consider the role of both the teacher and the SENCO within the graduated approach. The graduated approach is the four part cycle which is implemented to ensure that needs are identified and barriers to learning are removed, with decisions systematically being revisited. Table 5.1 summarises, from the SEND Code of Practice (DfE and DoH, 2015, pp. 92–103), the different roles.

Table 5.1 Role of the SENCO and the teachers

The graduated approach	Role of the teacher (class or subject)	Role of the SENCO
Assess	The class or subject teachers should carry out a full analysis of the child's needs.	The SENCO should support the teacher in this activity.
Plan	The teacher and the SENCO should agree with the parents, in consultation, the approach determined to support the child, including adjustments, interventions and support. The team should also share the expectations from the support. For example, academic and/or social, once the support is in place.	
		All teachers and support staff should be made aware of the pupil's needs as well as planned support and intended outcomes of support.
Do	The class or subject teacher should remain responsible for working with the child on a day-to-day basis. The class or subject teachers should work clearly to support staff with planning support, as well as assessing the impact of intervention. Teachers should also plan for how interventions can be linked to the classroom.	The SENCO should support the class/subject teacher re further assessment of the child's strength and areas of difficulty, to support problem solving and to advise on the effective implementation of support.
Review	The class or subject teacher should review the support in place, and the impact of this support, in light of the pupils progress and development, in consultation with the pupil and the parents.	The SENCO should work with the teacher to enable the review stage.

Source: SEND Code of Practice (2015, Ch. 6, pp. 92–103)

Something to think about

- How do teachers in your school know what their role is in relation to identifying and supporting learners with SEN?
- How do teachers in your school know the role of the SENCO in relation to identifying and supporting learners with SEN?
- Where is this stated in school and how can they refer to it?
- How often is the SEN policy/SEN information report referred to or read by colleagues working in school?
- Do you think teachers are aware of the documents and would they benefit from an easily 'digestible' version?

Later in the chapter we will explore ways in which you can emphasise and demonstrate the clarity between roles and responsibilities in school.

Once role and responsibilities have been established, it is important to consider the practical ways in which you can support colleagues in school. The aim here is twofold. Through a whole-school approach, you can begin to focus on developing inclusive practice, strategically, across your setting. However, in addition to this, moving towards a more structured approach to supporting colleagues will not only develop their own skills and capacity as teachers of children with SEN, but will also support you as a SENCO moving away from the role of 'SENCO as rescue', as suggested by Kearns (2005, p. 139). This reflects a more strategic view of support. This is not to suggest that the role will move away from being responsive, the very nature of the role means that you will be required to change plans, adapt and react to specific unplanned situations. Yet, as Rosen-Webb suggests, it is about the SENCO being able to balance 'on the job' activity, strategic thinking and planning proactively, as well as 'fire-fighting reactively' (2011, p. 166).

Leading and supporting colleagues: a whole-school approach

The following section outlines a number of activities and processes which you can implement in school to lead and support colleagues. The section contains longer-term, more strategic activities, alongside what might be considered 'quick wins'. I would advocate taking the same approach to implementing any of the activities below as you would when you receive an external agency report for a child; identify your top three activities which would address your most pressing concerns, implement and review before trying out further ideas. The previous chapter looked at how you can develop a SEN development plan. Some of the suggestions below may help with the practical execution of these aims, but equally you can use the development plan to stagger how you will implement these activities, as well as monitor impact.

Understanding your staff needs

Resources are a pressing issue within the world of SEN provision. Pearson and colleagues (2015) predicted that resources would decrease as a result of the SEND reforms, despite the assertion by Edward Timpson (DfE, 2014a), the then Parliamentary Under Secretary of State for Children and Families, that no child should lose their support as a result of the SEND reforms. In a recent study by the National Association of Head Teachers (NAHT, 2018) only 2% of respondents reported that the additional funding they received for children with Education, Health and Care (EHC) plans was enough to sufficiently meet the individual's needs. In addition to this, 73% of respondents stated that cuts to mainstream funding has meant that it is harder to support pupils with SEN, with 94% stating that it was harder to resource the support presently required than it was two years ago.

In today's economic climate, whether we are talking about time or money, resources are under pressure. In a school environment this means that the SENCO may be tasked with doing more with less. As such it is important to understand what resources you currently have, and a major resource you do have is your current staff. Before you begin to consider where to invest time and money, it is imperative to understand the need and skills of your staff. Therefore, the following whole-school activities may help you ascertain the current situation within your school.

- Carry out an audit of experience and skills with all staff. A quick survey, either paper-based or online, of staff can find out:
  - The training that staff have accessed and in what area. This may relate to short professional courses, or longer-term training, for example Masters level dyslexia training.
  - Their experiences of working with specific needs.
  - Their confidence levels in terms of supporting high incidence SEN. A quick Likert scale asking staff to rate their levels of confidence in relation to dyslexia, dyscalculia, ASD etc.

Ideas in action

Phoebe had been appointed as a SENCO in a new school. Since she was new to the role and the school, she did not know the staff, or what training they had accessed. She devised a short, paper-based questionnaire which

---

she gave out at the start of a staff meeting to enable her to gain an overview of the staff. She asked:

- What their role was e.g. midday supervisor/teaching assistant, teacher, SLT etc.
- Whether they had been on any specific SEN-focused training, what it was and when it occurred.
- What specific experience of teaching children with SEN they had.
- How confident they felt regarding their knowledge and understanding of strategies related to dyslexia, dyscalculia, ASD, speech and language, and attachment.
- What training in the area of SEN they would like in the next year.
- Whether they would like some initial individual support.

Phoebe found out that:

- Several teaching assistants had been training in a specific literacy intervention, but this intervention was not currently running.
- The majority of staff felt confident regarding identifying dyslexic-type difficulties and strategies to support this area.
- The majority wanted additional support regarding strategies to support children on the autism spectrum.
- A teacher in Year 6 had undertaken a part-time Masters degree in the autism spectrum: supporting children two years ago.
- The midday supervisors had not accessed any formal in-school training for 18 months.

As a response, Phoebe:

- Decided to find out if there was a need in the school to run the intervention. She could then either a) look at putting the intervention in place or b) log the training as a potential intervention which could be offered as and when required.
- Discussed with the Year 6 teacher the possibility of working together to compile some interim resources to support teachers, prior to arranging any more formal whole-school training.
- Arranged termly one hour meetings for midday supervisors where information and strategies could be shared regarding specific children.
- Liaised with the SLT to find out who was invited to whole-school in-service training days (INSET) and whether this could be broadened out to include all staff, when appropriate.

In addition to an audit of staff training, a learning walk or a series of observations of staff can provide you with valuable information regarding not only how to support staff, but also their strengths and/or how they can support you. Time is the key issue here, activities such as observations or learning walks can be pushed to the bottom of the pile because there is not enough time; direct consequences do not occur if these activities do not happen. Yet, in the longer term this can save time and energy and can be incredibly useful. You can use observations and/or learning walks to:

- Identify good practice in your school to share across departments.
- Establish a baseline of what quality teaching looks like in your school.
- Develop your own bank of strategies and good ideas, which you can disseminate to staff.
- Determine teaching pairs who 'buddy up' to support each other.
- Identify any themes or patterns across the school which may require support.

Nationally, the pattern regarding assessment and data is changing at a rapid pace. Perhaps the biggest change in recent times has been the removal of national curriculum levels and the introduction of the new National Curriculum (DfE, 2014b), which was introduced on the same day as the revised SEND Code of Practice (DfE and DoH, 2015). In your role as SENCO you will, no doubt, be familiar with data and using this to identify potential challenges individuals may be experiencing, as well as monitor the progress of individuals. However, you can also use data to look for patterns across the school. When you are reviewing data, you can look beyond an individual sense and use the data to help you effectively identify patterns so you can:

- improve teaching and learning;
- influence the strategic development of SEN policy and practice;
- indicate where an intervention is required or if an intervention is having an impact;
- impact on decisions about the deployment of SEN resources;
- indicate the need for specialist service input;
- identify vulnerable groups that overlap – boys with SEN, girls who are looked-after children (LAC);
- identify any trends over the last three years; and
- identify early any pupils who may have a SEN.

This will enable you to:

- evaluate if the strategies and approaches being used to remove barriers to learning are having an impact;
- determine what good progress for SEND pupils looks like in the school;
- ensure that there is a consistency of progress across the school;

- ensure that the school is 'narrowing the gap' between SEN and non-SEN pupils; and
- compare the school's SEN pupil performance with that of other schools, both locally and nationally.

In terms of leading and supporting colleagues, this will then enable you to determine the support that you will be able to give to individual teachers, year groups and subjects, either directly or via outside agencies.

Responding to identified staff needs

The information that you have gathered from the audit, the observation/learning walks and the data can then be used in a variety of ways. For the purposes of this chapter we are going to consider the types of activities you can try to respond to the needs you have identified. You can use the information to:

- Plan longer-term CPD. You can identify if there are specific areas of CPD needed, for example, if 80% of your staff have identified dyslexia as an area that they do not feel confident with, yet you have identified that this accounts for 60% of identified need in school, this may then become a whole-school priority. The next section will look at ways in which you can deliver CPD.
- Identify specific groups which may require more targeted support from the SENCO. Does the audit illustrate any specific patterns, such as within certain departments or phases which require more of your targeted support? For example, is there a specific year group which have identified a particular need? You can then think about targeting your time and resources there. This can take the form of mini CPD, online training or support with intervention and planning.
- Identify if there are any colleagues who would benefit from more targeted support.
- Identify strengths in the school using the audit and draw upon these resources. For example, if you have a member of staff who has attended additional dyslexia training and has rated themselves confident in this area, you can advise staff to speak to them for hints and tips (with their permission of course!). This could lead to the development of a system of mutual support where you match colleagues up who would benefit from support in specific areas. This could take the form of observing colleagues to develop ideas for strategies, support with planning, or with working with parents.
- Identify specific areas for support and longer-term planning by looking at the data patterns. Are there specific cohorts which currently concern you, perhaps with a higher percentage of SEN? Consider the short- and longer-term support this cohort receives and target resources, both human and physical, appropriately. This may also form part of the wider-school planning for staff deployment.

Create opportunities for development

Part of responding to staff needs is to ensure that there are opportunities, both formal and informal, for staff development. Typically, this might take the form of CPD during an INSET day or twilight session. It is imperative that teachers, both those in training and those practising, receive CPD regarding SEN and inclusive practice, to ensure that class and subject teachers are meeting the requirements of the national curriculum (DfE, 2014b) and the SEND Code of Practice (DfE and DoH, 2015) to respond to the needs of all learners. As stated by Gibson and Haynes (2009), to develop inclusive environments teachers need a clear understanding of their pupils and methods to support them. As Carter (2015) has highlighted, there is an urgent need to improve on the minimum requirement for teachers' SEN training within initial teacher training (ITT) (DfE, 2011), echoing earlier calls made by Golder et al. (2005). However, these are all future possibilities which will take time to come into effect and will not address the training needs in the short term – a potential issue for the current training available for teachers. SENCOs may find that they are required to provide *more* training and advice to colleagues regarding the provision of high quality teaching to meet the needs of all learners, particularly those who are new to the profession. Therefore, as a SENCO, you will need to consider how to provide CPD in your school against a backdrop of austerity.

- Consider the way in which CPD is delivered. SENCOs I have worked with have created 'mini CPD drop-in sessions' where they have spent 15 minutes or so, after school, looking at one specific area of SEN. This is voluntary, but content has been made available on shared drives for all staff. It might also be worth asking your staff the way in which they would like CPD to be delivered. Is there a place in school for online CPD? Look at free, online training provided by organisations such as nasen.
- Target specific groups. Training does not have to involve the whole school. Can you work with specific groups and/or departments who would benefit the most from your time? Or the time of others?
- Look at your networks, especially if you are working within a multi-academy trust. Is there another SENCO whose experience you could draw upon to deliver CPD to your school? In times of limited resources, we need to look at how we can support each other. Can you share your expertise across your networks?
- Consider a bulletin for SEN, via email. The bulletin can contain information specific to the school, for example, do staff know how many children in your school have additional needs? You can also have a termly focus on one area of high incidence SEN, including quick tips. Think about how to present this – avoid attachments, they won't be opened!

Create different avenues of support

There are various ways in which you can offer support to staff, which can be both proactive and reactive. Consider some of the ways in which you can provide support to staff, through providing opportunities for them to share their concerns.

- A 'drop in' surgery. Can you have a time after school, periodically, when teachers can pop in and ask you any quick SEN related questions?
- Introducing a SEN notice board in the staff room. You can use the notice board to put up general information regarding SEN, including processes, for staff. Note, this should not contain individual information.

Ideas in action

Aim:

To increase staff awareness of specific areas of SEN, to build on recently attended whole-school CPD.

Action:

Create a notice board in the staff room specifically for information related to SEN. Information to include:

- A visual overview of the process of Assess, Plan, Do, Review, illustrating the various roles within this.
- 'Top tip' of the week related to the recent CPD.
- Information re timings of SENCO surgeries.
- Pouch of referral forms for staff to use when they have a concern regarding a pupil (see 'Process, process, process' section below).

- Creating a process map which shows avenues of support. You can draw upon the people you have identified, through your audit, as having training and expertise in specific areas. The process can be a simplified version of the Assess, Plan, Do, Review process, which can not only indicate the processes to be followed, and by whom, but also indicate the supportive role of the SENCO throughout.
- Consider creating a reference guide of high incidence SEN, which staff can use as a quick guide. This is not to replace specific advice but could be another way in which you can support staff in their professional development.

Something to think about

Later in the book, Chapter 7, 'Managing your role: challenges and opportunities', explores ways in which you can develop your team and the network around you to support you in your role. The creation of resources is one way in which this can happen.

I have had lots of SENCOs say that they are going to create quick strategy sheets for specific areas of high incidence SEN, to give to staff as a quick reference guide. Something which they create themselves.

However, if you are in a SENCO network, a multi-academy trust, or you are completing your NA SENCO, is this something you could divide and conquer as a team? You could take one area each and then pool all your resources to create the ultimate guide.

Be a translator

In education, in general, we tend to talk in acronyms, and I suspect that in SEN this is even more prominent. The challenge is that this can become part of our everyday language, to the point where we don't even realise that we are talking in another language. For example, could you translate this sentence for a teacher or a parent:

> We need to speak to the LA as we think the pupil needs an EHCP. I will arrange a TAF, but we need to involve the EP and think about SALT and the progress they have made towards the ILOs.

Later in the book we will look at the impact that this can have on parents, however this can also be confusing for teachers – and SENCOs! Therefore, think about how you can act as a translator for the people you work with.

- Create an acronym handout (see Appendix). Display this on the notice board or attach to every report.
- Earlier we talked about the SEN policy and the SEN information report – who these are written for and how often they are referred to. Consider the information in your SEN policy – what do teachers need to know, and how can it be condensed for them?
- Reports from outside agencies can be overwhelming. They tend to be long, through necessity, and the translation of the reports can be problematic depending on the level of technical language used. Therefore, look at ways in which you can distil

the key information from outside agency reports so that the key messages reach the correct staff. This can be time consuming. If you are commissioning an outside agency to undertake a report, make a request that, alongside the detailed report, they create a one-page overview, highlight key strengths and areas to develop, and the key strategies to try.

- Later in the book we will look at how you can support parents with reports. However, a 'debrief meeting' with the teachers concerned can be a quick way to ensure that they have accessed the report and understand the content. It is advisable to ensure that the report is shared with the teacher prior to the meeting, so that they have a chance to raise any questions. If you are able to set up a meeting or phone call with the external agency directly with the teacher, even better. However, ensure that you are compliant with your information sharing policies in school.

Process, process, process

I am big on processes, it helps keeps things in order, gives shape and consistency. Developing your own processes, which suit your context, can do the same. This can be particularly helpful for supporting colleagues regarding their specific role within SEN provision; they see where they fit within the wider process of SEN, which can sometimes be confusing. Consider some of the following and how these can potentially support your environment:

- A referral process for teachers to share their concerns. It is essential to have a system in place so teachers can effectively share their concerns, in a timely manner, but also to enable review and reflection on these concerns. This is an imperative part of the Assess, Plan, Do, Review process. When I was a SENCO, one of the key things I found hard was when teachers would stop me, in the corridor or at the start of a meeting, to share a concern or worry they had, 'Can I just mention to you Sam, I think he has dyslexic tendencies.' The issue here is that I then had to do something with this concern, in essence, the concern had been passed on to me. This then, consciously or not, can shift the responsibility to the SENCO, rather than the teacher, which as detailed above does not correlate with the SEND Code of Practice (DfE and DoH, 2015). Therefore, consider a way in which you can manage these conversations so that you are able to support teachers effectively, whilst also ensuring that the responsibility lays firmly with them.
- One way of doing this is to have an internal referral form where teachers can share their concerns with you, but, equally, this enables them to share with you what they have done. A number of SENCOs I have worked with have developed this form so that it also acts as a prompt for ideas of support.

Ideas in action

When creating a one-page referral form, you can use this to 'nudge' teachers to think about what they should be doing. Each form will need to be designed to suit each context. However, you might want to think about including the following:

- Name of child.
- Nature of concern.
- How long the teacher has been concerned.
- What strategies/interventions have they tried? (You might want to include a list here of quality first teaching strategies you might expect to see in the class, to act as a prompt).
- Which worked and which didn't? (Encourage reflecting!)
- What do the parents think?
- What does the pupil think?
- Proposed next steps.

This document can then be used not only as a record of the Assess, Plan, Do, Review process, but can also serve as a prompt to teachers about who should be involved, and when.

Getting staff on board

One of the key challenges in school can be trying to get 'everyone on board'. Within school, there are constant demands placed upon teachers' time, whether this is the challenge of the everyday, the way specific times throughout the year can bring added pressure, or the introduction of new initiatives. One of the challenges for a SENCO can be that you feel like you are adding to the challenge, through asking staff to engage in new processes or procedures. Or as one SENCO I worked with said, 'I am literally adding on another layer of misery'.

One of the criticisms of SEN policy is that it seems to sit outside of the wider, educational agenda. Glazzard (2014) suggests that the advancement of inclusive policy is already problematic, in part due to the tension between the inclusion agenda and the standards agenda (Ellis and Tod, 2014; Norwich, 2014). As discussed in the earlier chapters, part of the challenge for the SENCO is how to advocate for SEN policy amongst a wider backdrop of seemingly competing, or at the very least incompatible, policies. As such it is important to develop a consistent, unrelenting message regarding the central importance of SEN and inclusive practice.

However, the alternative view is that through developing new processes and procedures you are developing your staff's skills and capacity and, as a consequence, you are improving inclusive practice in your school, which will benefit everyone in the long run. Yet, due to the demands placed upon teachers, you will need to consider how to get staff on board and engaging with you as quickly as possible.

- Always pilot new ideas. Within research, before being let loose on participants, we need to test out our data-gathering instruments, whether this be questionnaires, interviews or observations for example. It enables the researcher to carry out a 'live test' and to get honest feedback on the process. It saves a lot of time and can be incredibly insightful when someone is able to provide you with honest feedback. The same can be said of all new SEN processes in school. If you are seeking to introduce a new mentoring system, or you are looking to introduce referral paperwork, test this out with some trusted colleagues. Ask them for their feedback and incorporate this into your final version. This means that, hopefully, any issues that may crop up will be immediately dealt with before you release the ideas to the whole school, but it also gives you an extra voice which can say to the wider staff, 'Yes, I've tried it, it works'.

- The role of the SENCO can be a lonely job, therefore, it is essential to build your network wherever possible. When you are developing new ideas, processes or even creating your SEN development plan, ensure that these activities are not conducted in isolation. It might be appropriate to invite colleagues to join a working party or invite them to comment on a proposal or a piece of work. The outcome is threefold: you are sharing the breadth and depth of your role; you are ensuring colleagues are involved; and you are further highlighting the importance and prominence of SEN within your school.

- Consider developing a team of 'SEN and inclusion' champions. Consider who you can work with to ensure that the subject of SEN and inclusion is raised at every meeting. For example, who can advocate for SEN and inclusion in departmental meetings when you are not there? This can be as simple as someone raising the issue and inviting comment.

- Drip feed – what language is used and where? Are you using phrases in your documentation such as 'family leadership', 'family collaboration' or 'outcome focused'? A review of documents to check that the language used is consistent can be helpful. For example, is person-first terminology used throughout all school documentation? This means that in your policies you refer to 'children with SEN' rather than 'SEN children', or 'individuals on the autism spectrum' rather than 'autistic children'.

The above strategies can be used across the whole school. However, specific groups may need specific support at specific times. The following section looks at support for specific groups, however the ideas within this section are not restricted to these groups.

Leading and supporting specific groups

New starters at your school

Starting any new job is daunting and exhausting! You are trying to get to grips with not only the role, but the new people, the challenges and also the processes. Things are done differently everywhere! To this end it can be useful to think about what new starters need to know when they come to your school.

- Ask a relatively new starter at your school what they wish they had known when they had started at your school – use this information to create an induction pack. The induction pack can contain key information for new starters, particularly in relation to processes in your school. You might include:
  - A teacher friendly version of the school's SEN policy (plus original as an appendices).
  - An overview of the graduated approach and how it is applied in your setting.
  - An acronym handout (see Appendix).
  - An overview of who is who in the school and who oversees which area (in relation to SEN).
  - A 'what to do when I'm concerned' sheet – indicating the processes.
  - A blank referral form.
  - One-page high incidence SEN information sheets.

- Consider allocating a mentor upon joining to whom the new starter can go to, if they can't access the SENCO, for guidance and support. The earlier audit of skills and experience, alongside the observations, may help you identify specific mentors.
- Arrange catch ups scheduled in to the term so you can review how things are going.
- Ensure the skills and experience audit is completed to enable you to determine individual support, as well as feeding this into the whole-school audit.

Newly qualified teachers

As highlighted earlier, you may find that you need to provide additional support to newly qualified teachers (NQTs) regarding their development of their SEN and inclusive practice. Whilst this may form part of their NQT year, a focus from the SENCO in this area can be helpful and illustrate that CPD is long term and ongoing.

- Share with them the induction pack.
- Get the NQTs together – share top tips (and stresses).

- Allocate a mentor to whom the NQT can go to for additional support and advice in relation to SEN-specific issues.
- Carve out time for observations – where the NQT can observe their own class. Make arrangements for the NQT class to be covered so that they can observe their own class in action. Meet with the NQT afterwards so they can share what they observed and you can plan next steps for the pupils. If possible, observe together.
- Arrange a time for the NQT to observe other classes, to observe good practice with a specific focus on quality first teaching.
- Arrange planning support so the NQT can discuss their plans with you, or their mentor, with a specific focus on quality first teaching.

Support staff

As highlighted earlier, support staff have increased in number and typically tend to support individuals or children with additional needs (Blatchford et al., 2009). Support staff are a key and vital resource for SENCOs. As such it is imperative to think about how they are supported in school.

- What information do the support staff in your school have access to? This is where the SEN notice board and whole-school email bulletin can be a useful method of ensuring everyone accesses communicated information.
- Ensure that support staff also contribute to the audit of staff skills and experience so that you can plan for future training.
- Create a space so that there can be regular meetings of all support staff. This can be used to communicate key messages, conduct mini CPD or be a general catch up.
- Consider how support staff and teachers communicate. What mechanisms are in place? Refer back to the SEND Code of Practice (DfE and DoH, 2015) to remind staff that the children remain the responsibility of the teacher. It is better to have one less support session, so that support can be properly planned, rather than for-going an opportunity for liaison.
- Consider how support staff are inducted. We are asking support staff to work, often one-to-one, with some of our most vulnerable children. How are staff supported with understanding what their role is?
- Consider utilising some of the suggestions for NQTs, such as observations and buddying up, to help new support staff to your school.
- Undertaking one-to-one or small-group support is hard. It is intense and often support staff may find themselves in challenging situations. What systems do you have in place for support after situations have occurred? Often debrief sessions are focused on the child, rightly so, so that antecedents can be identified and

future support offered, but, equally, it is important to offer debrief sessions to the support staff to enable them to process some of the situations they find themselves in.

In summary

The activities detailed above are specifically designed to offer a practical approach to leading and supporting colleagues in a strategic manner, with a view to trying to move away from the firefighting version of the SENCO. Naturally this will always occur, but it is not a desirable, permanent state. The main factor which is likely to impact on you being able to facilitate these activities is time. As such, it may be that the SENCO finds themselves in a position of not being able to undertake longer-term, development activities. However, I would urge you to think about carving out and protecting some time for at least one or two of these activities to test out the potential impact on your team. Later in the book we will be exploring ways in which you can manage your time. However, by focusing on these activities you can begin to develop the capacity of your staff, and as a consequence, change the focus of your time.

Something to think about

Reflect back on the priorities you have identified for your school.

What two activities could you undertake from the list above in support of the development of your priorities?

Remember, treat this chapter as a toolbox. Choose a small number of activities or strategies, try out and reflect.

References

Blatchford, P., Bassett, P., Brown, P. and Webster, R. (2009) 'The effect of support staff on pupil engagement and individual attention', *British Educational Research Journal*, 35 (5), pp. 661–686.

Carter, A. (2015) *Carter review of Initial Teacher Training (ITT)*. Available at: www.gov.uk/government/uploads/system/uploads/attachment_data/file/399957/Carter_Review.pdf (Accessed 5th May 2016).

Cole, B. A. (2005) 'Mission Impossible? Special educational needs, inclusion and the re-conceptualisation of the role of the SENCo in England and Wales', *European Journal of Special Needs Education*, 20 (3), pp. 287–307.

Department for Education (DfE). (2011) *Teachers' standards: Guidance for school leaders, school staff and governing bodies*. Available at: www.gov.uk/government/uploads/system/uploads/attach ment_data/file/301107/Teachers__Standards.pdf (Accessed 10th March 2015).

Department for Education (DfE). (2014a) *Parents feel more supported ahead of radical SEND reforms*. [Press Release]. 15th August 2014. Available at: www.gov.uk/government/news/parents-feel-more-supported-ahead-of-radical-send-reforms (Accessed 1st September 2014).

Department for Education (DfE). (2014b) *National curriculum in England: framework for key stages 1 to 4*. Available at: www.gov.uk/government/publications/national-curriculum-in-england-frame work-for-key-stages-1-to-4/the-national-curriculum-in-england-framework-for-key-stages-1-to-4 (Accessed 4th September 2014).

Department for Education (DfE) and Department of Health (DoH). (2015) *Special educational needs and disability Code of Practice: 0–25 years*. Available at: www.gov.uk/government/uploads/ system/uploads/attachment_data/file/398815/SEND_Code_of_Practice_January_2015.pdf (Accessed 1st February 2015).

Ellis, S. and Tod, J. (2014) 'Chapter 5. Special educational needs and inclusion: reflection, renewal and reality', *Journal of Research in Special Educational Needs*, 14 (3), pp. 205–210.

Gibson, S. and Haynes, J. (eds.) (2009) *Perspectives on participation and inclusion: engaging education*. London: Continuum.

Glazzard, J. (2014) 'The standards agenda: reflections of a special educational needs co-ordinator', *Support for Learning*, 29 (1), pp. 39–53.

Golder, G., Norwich, B. and Bayliss, P. (2005) 'Preparing teachers to teach pupils with special educational needs in more inclusive schools: evaluating a PGCE development', *British Journal of Special Education*, 32 (2), pp. 92–99.

Kearns, H. (2005) 'Exploring the experiential learning of special educational needs coordinators', *Journal of In-Service Education*, 31 (1), pp. 131–150.

National Association of Headteachers (NAHT). (2018) *Empty promises: The crisis in supporting children with SEND*. Available at: www.naht.org.uk/news-and-opinion/news/funding-news/ empty-promises-the-crisis-in-supporting-children-with-send/ (Accessed 3rd January 2019)

Norwich, B. (2014) 'Changing policy and legislation and its effects on inclusive and special education: a perspective from England', *British Journal of Special Education*, 41 (4), p. 40.

Pearson, S., Mitchell, R. and Rapti, M. (2015) 'I will be "fighting" even more for pupils with SEN: SENCOs' role predictions in the changing English policy context', *Journal of Research in Special Educational Needs*, 15 (1), pp. 48–56.

Rosen-Webb, S. (2011) 'Nobody tells you how to be a SENCo', *British Journal of Special Education*, 38 (4), pp. 159–168.

Developing relationships
Pupils and parents

Introduction

One of the most significant changes that the introduction of the 2014 Children and Families Act, and related guidance, brought about was the increased focus on the support and involvement of children, young people and their families with regards to the SEN system. The 2014 Children and Families Act states that a local authority must have regard to four areas:

- The views, wishes and feelings of the child and their parents, or the young person.
- The importance of participation, as fully as possible, in decision making.
- The importance of being provided with support and information to enable participation in decision making.
- The need to support the child and parents, or young person, to help achieve the best possible educational and other outcomes.

The SEND Code of Practice (DfE and DoH, 2015), which provides the statutory guidance regarding the duties, policies and procedures of the 2014 Children and Families Act, is based on principles that seek to create a system which is outcome focused and aspirational, with children and families at the centre. The underlying aim is that the new system should be less confrontational and adversarial. The role of children, young people and parents/carers are central to the guidance, which throughout states the need for collaboration and involvement between all parties. The development of these principles is rooted within a history which has documented the issues children and families have experienced when negotiating the SEN system (DCFS, 2009). This frustration with the previous system was evident during the process of consultation prior to the introduction of the SEND reforms. The Green Paper at the time, *Support and Aspiration: A New Approach to Special Educational Needs and Disability, a Consultation*, stated that:

- Disabled children and children with SEN tell us that they can feel frustrated by a lack of the right help at school or from other services.
- Parents say that the system is bureaucratic, bewildering and adversarial and that it does not sufficiently reflect the needs of their child and their family life.

- The system to support children and young people who are disabled or who have SEN often works against the wishes of families.

(DfE, 2012, p. 4)

The SEND Code of Practice (DfE and DoH, 2015) details how children, young people and families should be involved in the child's education as well as specifically detailing the processes to enable this. As such, it is imperative that SENCOs create an ethos through specific systems, processes and expectations to foster meaningful pupil and parent relationships in their school. However, over and above meeting statutory obligations, increased collaboration and engagement between all parties can bring a significant number of benefits to all, especially the children who are in receipt of special educational provision.

Yet, for a SENCO this can mean that there are challenges to be addressed. Challenges may relate to how to work effectively with pupils and parents in a meaningful way, how to engage and inspire teachers and colleagues to do the same, how to ensure consistency across the setting and, equally, how to work with individuals who, due to a host of reasons, may feel disconnected, disenfranchised and lack confidence in *the system.*

As such, the focus of the SENCO role moves beyond one which puts into place systems and processes, towards one which seeks to develop effective working relationships with children, young people and families. The SENCO may find that they are advocating on behalf of children and families, or putting in place systems to increase their participation. Ultimately, the SENCO role is one which needs to seek ways in which children, young people and families can be advocated for in order to help secure the very best outcomes for children and young people in an inclusive environment. It is through advocacy, and specifically the development of relationships, that parties can begin to work effectively together.

This chapter will begin by looking at the policy context which directly relates to the increased focus on pupil and parent collaboration within the area of special educational needs. The chapter will consider the benefits that an increased collaboration can bring, for children, young people, their families, as well as for teachers and the inclusive ethos within the school. The chapter will then consider the potential barriers which may adversely impact on the development of relationships with pupils and parents, before looking at ways in which pupil and parents can be supported, through increased collaboration and advocacy, at both a whole-school and individual level.

The chapter will explore the idea of developing relationships in the broadest sense. This will include the idea of advocacy, noting that advocacy is broad and means different things in different contexts. Heitin describes advocacy as 'to speak or plead the case of another' (2013, p. 43). The purpose of the SENCO is not just to speak on the behalf of others, but to create an environment through which multiple views and multiple voices, including that of pupils and parents, can be shared, heard and valued concurrently. Therefore, whilst the strategies suggested, or questions posed, in this chapter have been developed to encourage and support relationships, the strategies also consider how increased communication can be the cornerstone of a good relationship. Therefore, terms including communication, relationships, collaboration, involvement, advocacy and support have been used throughout this chapter; all of which reflect the underlying principles of the SEND Code of Practice (DfE and DoH, 2015).

For ease of reference, the chapter will look at the aspects of working with pupils and working with parents separately, with strategies listed under whole-school and individual approaches. In addition to this, similar to the previous chapter, I would encourage you to think about this chapter as a tool box. Consider your SEN development plan and whether any of these suggestions would help you in meeting your aims. Pick two or three and return to the toolbox at a later date.

In summary this chapter focuses on:

- children and families at the centre: the policy context;
- pupil relationships: why these are important;
- family relationships: why these are important;
- are you meeting the SEND Code of Practice guidance?;
- an awareness of potential barriers;
- pupil relationships: whole-school approaches;
- pupil relationships: individual approaches;
- family relationships: whole-school approaches;
- family relationships: individual approaches;
- specific circumstances: Education, Health and Care plans; and
- it's not always going to go how you planned.

Children and families at the centre: the policy context

The SEND Code of Practice (DfE and DoH, 2015) is underpinned by three key principles. The principles state that local authorities, when executing their statutory functions in relation to children and young people with SEND, must have regard to:

- the views, wishes and feelings of the child or young person, and the child's parents;
- the importance of the child or young person, and the child's parents, participating as fully as possible in decisions, and being provided with the information and support necessary to enable participation in those decisions; and

- the need to support the child or young person, and the child's parents, in order to facilitate the development of the child or young person and to help them achieve the best possible educational and other outcomes, preparing them effectively for adulthood.

(DfE and DoH, 2015, p. 19)

The SEND Code of Practice (DfE and DoH, 2015) states that the overarching aims are for children to:

- achieve their best;
- become confident individuals living fulfilling lives; and
- make a successful transition into adulthood, whether into employment, further or higher education or training.

To achieve these aims, schools must use 'their best endeavours' (DfE and DoH, 2015, p. 92) to ensure children receive the provision they need. Furthermore, it is through engagement with children, young people and their families, through a holistic, cohesive approach, that these aims can be realised.

The SEND Code of Practice (DfE and DoH, 2015) is emphatic that there needs to be an increased focus on the participation of the individual in decision making, and greater cooperation between education, health and social care (Lauchlan and Greig, 2015). Notably, the SEND Code of Practice states that the involvement of children and young people in decision making should be 'at individual and strategic levels' (DfE and DoH, 2015, p. 14), a principle which is reflected, in part, in the introduction of personal budgets, which enables the young person or parent/carers to be involved in securing provision, via direct access to funding. In relation to this, one of the changes to the guidance is the increased focus on 'high aspirations and on improving outcomes for children and young people' (NASEN, 2015, p. 3). This reflects the increased focus on person-centred planning within the revised SEND Code of Practice (Norwich, 2017).

Such a position has been paramount from the beginning of the SEND reforms; terms such as *cooperate* and *communicate* have been replaced with *coproduce*, with the SEND Code of Practice stating that this term means that parents should 'feel they have participated fully in the process and have a sense of co-ownership' (DfE and DoH, 2015, p. 61). However, to understand the principles in action it is imperative to return to the SEND Code of Practice (DfE and DoH, 2015) to explore how coproduction can be specifically enacted. Ultimately, it is about viewing parents and families as equal partners, with the SEND Code of Practice stating, 'Parents know their children best and it is important that all professionals listen and understand when parents express concerns about their child's development' (DfE and DoH, 2015, p. 85).

Chapter 6 of the SEND Code of Practice (DfE and DoH, 2015) provides more specific detail regarding the involvement of children, young people and their families. For example, section 6.19 in the SEND Code of Practice states, in relation to identifying SEN in schools, that whilst gathering information informally and making a considered decision as to whether a child may have special educational needs, the view of the pupils and their families should also be collected. Later, within the explanation of the Assess, Plan, Do, Review process, the SEND Code of Practice states that when deciding to make additional provision through SEN support, parents must be formally informed, noting that 'parents should have already been involved in forming the assessment of needs' (DfE and DoH, 2015, p. 101).

Pupil relationships: why these are important

There are many arguments as to the importance of developing effective working relationships with pupils. Perhaps central to this relationship is the development of pupil voice within the school setting. Flutter would argue that pupil voice is 'nested within the broader principle of pupil participation, a term which embraces strategies that offer pupil opportunities for active involvement in decision making within their schools' (2007, p. 344). It could be argued that the rationale can fall into two camps: children's rights and positive impact on the individual.

In terms of children's rights, The United Nations Convention on the Rights of the Child (UNCRC) (1989), article 12, states:

1. Parties shall assure to the child who is capable of forming his or her own views the right to express those views freely in all matters affecting the child, the views of the child being given due weight in accordance with the age and maturity of the child.
2. For this purpose, the child shall in particular be provided the opportunity to be heard in any judicial and administrative proceedings affecting the child, either directly, or through a representative or an appropriate body, in a manner consistent with the procedural rules of national law.

The SEND Code of Practice (DfE and DoH, 2015) is explicit throughout that children and young people's views must be sought, in alignment with the UNCRC. However, it is also worth considering the positive impact on the individual and the collective when relationships, specifically developing pupil voice, are prioritised.

Marsh is emphatic regarding the benefits to the individual and to the school stating, 'high levels of student engagement and motivation are undoubtedly key factors to ensuring that pupils thrive and succeed at school' (2012, p. 161). This idea reflects the four categories Whitty and Wisby present when arguing in favour for pupil voice:

- Children's rights.
- Active citizenship.
- School improvement.
- Personalisation.

(2007, p. 21)

Certainly, the SEND Code of Practice (DfE and DoH, 2015) states that a key part of identifying SEN in schools relates to how children respond to support, underlying the importance of asking the child what they think about the provision in place. Ultimately, whilst there are approaches that can be developed to support pupil collaboration and pupil voice in school, much of this relates to the type of relationship we foster with students, and the type of relationship we expect our teachers to foster, all of which relates to our view of an inclusive environment.

Family relationships: why these are important

In a similar way, developing partnerships with parents is not only a moral responsibility, but there can be a significant, positive impact on the individual and the family. Whilst the SEND Code of Practice (DfE and DoH, 2015) has brought about a renewed focus on this area, it is not new. In 1978, the Warnock Report highlighted the importance of working with parents, stating 'the successful education of children with special educational needs is dependent upon the full involvement of their parents' (DES, 1978, p. 150). The report later added that parents needed to be seen as equal partners. The Lamb Inquiry (DCFS, 2009) also highlighted the importance of the relationship with parents, stating that parents need good, honest communication.

It is important to think about the benefits which improved communication, and improved relationships, can bring. Harris and Goodall (2007, cited in Day, 2013) state that parental engagement in education makes a significant difference to the child's subsequent attainment. They further add that, 'there is a consistent relationship between increasing parental engagement (particularly of "hard to reach" parents) and improved attendance, behaviour and student achievement' (Harris and Goodall, 2007, cited in Day, 2013, p. 38). This is later echoed by Edwards who states, 'Parents are the key to unlocking learner potential' (2016, p. 124). However, it is important to view this information sharing as a two way process; parents are the expert on their child and teachers are the experts on education. Sharing experiences and insights can be hugely beneficial when planning special educational provision.

Therefore, this suggests that much is to be gained through the development of communication and relationships with parents, and the SENCO will be instrumental in not only developing direct relationships with parents, but also in supporting colleagues with this area.

Are you meeting the SEND Code of Practice guidance?

One of the first things you need to consider is how, in your setting, you meet the requirements of the SEND Code of Practice (DfE and DoH, 2015) in relation to working with children, young people and families. Chapter 6 of the SEND Code of Practice specifically details how and when to work with children, young people and families in schools. It is important, as a SENCO, that you refer back to this guidance, or the guidance which relates to your setting.

Table 6.1 has summarised the guidance in Chapter 6 which relates to SEN support (DfE and DoH, 2015, pp. 91–104). The number in brackets refers to the location of the guidance within the SEND Code of Practice.

Ideas in action

Read the chapter in the SEND Code of Practice (DfE and DoH, 2015) which is relevant to your setting. Highlight the specific times that parents must, and should, be involved, and how.

Refer back to your SEN policy, your SEN information report and your general processes in school.

Do you meet the requirements and the recommendations of the SEND Code of Practice?

An awareness of potential barriers

As a SENCO, you may have already decided to focus on the development of pupil and parent relationships as part of your longer term strategic plan. However, before you begin to implement new ideas, it is important to consider some of the factors which may be acting as existing barriers to changing or implementing practice. Day (2013) highlights the potential barriers which may impact on parental engagement, which

Table 6.1 The SEND Code of Practice summary of pupil–parent roles

	Involving children, young people and parents	Involving parents/carers
Schools must:	Ensure that they are actively involved in decision-making through the approaches set out [in Chapter 6] (6.69 and 6.7).	Inform parents when they are making special educational provision for a child (6.2). When it is decided that a pupil does have SEN, the pupil's parents must be formally informed that special educational provision is being made (6.43). Provide parents with an annual report on progress (6.64).
School should:	When gathering evidence regarding less than expected progress, views should be sought (6.19). When deciding whether to make special educational provision, the information gathering should include an early discussion with the pupil and their parents. Discussions should be holistic, including strengths and areas for developments, agreed outcomes and next steps (6.39). A note of early discussion should be put on the pupil's record and given to parents (6.39). Schools should share information about the local authority's Information, Advice and Support Service (6.39). A date for reviewing progress should be agreed (6.43). The graduated approach: At every stage, Assess, Plan, Do and Review, views should be sought. Adjustments, interventions and support should be agreed in consultation with the parents (6.48).	When professionals are not already working with school staff, the SENCO should contact them if the parents agree (6.47). The graduated approach: Parents should be fully aware of the planned support and intervention, and where appropriate, should seek parent's involvement to reinforce or contribute to progress at home (6.51). The information in 6.39 should be readily available to and discussed with the pupil's parents (6.51). Parents should have clear information about the impact of the support and interventions provided (6.55). The pupil's parents should always be involved in any decision to involve specialists. Outcomes of discussions should be shared with parents (6.59). When working with specialists, consideration should be given to approaches, strategies and interventions (6.62).

(*Continued*)

Table 6.1 (Cont.)

	Involving children, young people and parents	Involving parents/carers
	At the review stage, views should be sought, progress reviewed and changes to support and outcomes considered in consultation with the parent and pupil (6.54, 6.65, 6.70). Transition: Schools should agree with parents and pupils the information to be shared as part of the planning for transition (6.57).	When a pupil receives SEN support, the school should talk to parents regularly. This should be at least three times per year (6.65). These meetings may align with the normal cycle of parent meetings but should be longer (6.69). Review meetings should consider outcomes, action and support. The record should be given to the parents (6.71). This should be in an accessible format (6.75).
Additional guidance:	It is important that all professionals listen and understand when concerns are expressed – by parents or children and young people themselves (6.20).	

Source: DfE and DoH, 2015

include the parents' own experience of education, the parents' lack of understanding of the school and/or SEN system, their literacy levels, or their confidence in formal situations, such as meetings. In relation to this, there is the potential barrier of differing power dynamics between teachers and parents, as well as other professionals, and how this might impact on the pupils' or parents' feelings and their ability to contribute; as Whitty and Wisby (2007) explain, inviting views on pupils' learning can provide a challenge to the teachers' professionalism. However, equally, feedback can help teachers improve their practice by understanding the barriers as perceived by the pupils. All of these are aspects which we will address later in the chapter.

It is also important to think about the parents themselves, and the needs which they have. Being a parent to a child who has additional needs can be a lonely business. Feelings of isolation can result in the family not accessing activities or experiences which other 'typical' families experience. This may limit opportunities to meet other parents, particularly those who understand the position of a parent whose child has SEN. Whilst there may be opportunities to network with other parents at school or other contexts, parents whose children have additional needs may find this furthers feelings of isolation, as they may feel 'set apart' from others due to their experiences in relation to their child's needs. As such, it is important to consider how this may act as a barrier. Further barriers may occur due to the additional requirements placed upon the family by the school; these requirements may prove to be too much. Parents may be experiencing high levels of stress or anxiety.

Finally, we need to think about the impact that a renewed focus on developing relationships may have on pupils and parents. It is important to consider that engaging pupils may also bring tensions, including overburdening children with feeling related to decision-making (Norwich and Kelly, 2006). We could hypothesise that this is equally true for any contributor, including parents. Equally, we need to think about how we respond to pupils and parents, to ensure that we are moving beyond tokenistic engagement. Pupils and parents need to see value in engaging and contributing with school, rather than schools ticking a box. Therefore, we need to proceed carefully and consider how we can support pupils and parents in their engagement, rather than placing another, potentially burdensome, expectation on them.

Ultimately, it is important to remember that the responsibility for developing relationships with both pupils and parents remains with the professional (Hornby and Lafaele, 2011). It is perhaps useful to consider the development of the inclusive ethos within school as relating not only to including children, but all interested parties, including parents, and how, as a SENCO, you can work to develop this across the school.

Something to think about

It is worth bearing in mind that the pupils and families that you seek to work with bring with them not only a wealth of expertise, but also varying experiences.

You may be working with children who have previously shared their views on their provision and have come to realise that there is actually no point in sharing their views, as nothing ever changes. You may be working with parents who have had to work tirelessly to have their voice heard, who may feel that 'professionals' cannot be trusted, whether this be through their own experience of school or as a parent.

Therefore, it could be argued that the first role of the SENCO is to become a 'trusted listener'. The importance of trust between all parties cannot be overstated, but as a SENCO, the first challenge might be getting all parties on board and beginning to trust each other. Not over promising and under-delivering but ensuring that contributions from all parties are valued and recognised.

Pupil relationships: whole-school approaches

Whole-school audit

Perhaps one of the issues we need to consider when we are seeking to develop relationships with pupils who have additional needs is that we are immediately creating a separatist industry; we are considering what can be specially put in place for pupils with SEN. However, building on from the earlier chapter which looked at creating an inclusive ethos, perhaps the first consideration should be to look at what is already in place for all pupils, and how effectively this works for all. It is important to note that the SEND Code of Practice states that schools, 'must ensure that children and young people with SEN engage in the activities of the school alongside pupils who do not have SEN' (DfE and DoH, 2015, p. 92). Questions to consider include:

- How accessible are activities across the school for pupils with SEN?
- What mechanisms across the school are used to support pupil relationships, including ensuring pupils have a voice?
- How are children with SEN represented within these systems?
- Are specific adjustments required to make these systems more accessible? Or are additional, complimentary systems necessary?

It can also be interesting to audit school policy, and the processes for developing school policy. Particular policies of interest may be the SEN policy, assessment policies and behaviour policies. Questions to consider may include:

- Do the policies make specific reference to pupil relationships, for example the development of pupil voice?
- How do the policies specifically support the development of teacher–pupil relationships?
- Are children with additional needs specifically considered within the policies, particularly in terms of developing relationships?

However, over and above auditing processes and documents, one of the quickest ways to explore how children are feeling about their experience at your school is to ask them. This could be through:

- online surveys;
- focus groups;
- peer coaching; or
- individual interviews.

This does not have to be overly formal but can give you an immediate snapshot of what the pupils think is working well, and what they think isn't working well, in your school.

Training for staff

One of the key challenges for developing engagement in pupil voice is training for staff. Marsh (2012) listed five key areas which pupils identified as intrinsic to a positive relationship with their teacher:

- Friendly and flexible approach.
- Enthusiastic and engaging delivery.
- Noticing talent.
- Personal interactions.
- Effective classroom management.

In terms of developing relationships with pupils, it may be worth considering the areas where your staff may need support. For example, are your teachers concerned regarding what to 'do' with pupil voice. Teachers may be concerned that asking pupils for their opinion, or preferences, means they have to act upon it, regardless of the request! Staff may benefit from reassurances that listening to and noting preferences, wishes and related actions does not mean they have to act on them, but they do have to be considered as part of special educational provision arrangements.

Pupil relationships: individual approaches

Formal or informal contact?

The SEND Code of Practice (DfE and DoH, 2015) stipulates times when pupil's views must be sought, as detailed earlier in the chapter. However, it is important to consider how relationships are developed, and what insights these might lead to. For example, if the only times pupils' views are sought is during the annual review process, how meaningful are these opportunities? Think about ways in which pupils can informally share how they feel about school and their provision. This may be their key worker touching base with them on a weekly basis.

Pick your people

Think about who is the best person to develop a relationship with the pupils, this is particularly true for secondary schools where the number of teachers can bring an added complication. For example, if the person facilitating a pupil's annual contribution is also the person who provides a significant amount of support for the pupil, how are we enabling the pupil to give an honest response? A more neutral person might be appropriate. In some cases there might be an opportunity for peer to peer mentoring, where it may be appropriate for a senior pupil to work with a younger pupil.

Pick your times

In relation to the above points regarding the right person and the right form, it is important to think about the right time to engage with pupils. If you are seeking more formal views from the pupil, it may be appropriate to give them the topic/questions in advance, so they have thinking time.

Pick your medium

In addition to the point above, it is worthwhile thinking about the way in which pupil's want to respond. Would they prefer:

- a meeting;
- emailing responses;
- an online survey;
- drawing;
- using puppets; or
- a video.

Family relationships: whole-school approaches

Whole-school audit

In relation to conducting a whole-school audit of pupil relationships, it can equally be useful to apply the same premise for parental engagement. SENCOs who are new to the role or new to the school may find it particularly useful to find out:

- what provision there is in school to specifically encourage engagement with families in general; and
- whether there are any activities or opportunities specifically tailored for parents whose children have SEN.

Before introducing new ideas to support parent relationships with the school, it may be worth asking parents what they want. It can save you a lot of time and stop you directing your energies in the wrong direction. A simple paper-based or online survey can give you some basic information to work with, by asking:

- how long they have been at the school;
- the rating levels they would give for information/support/communication;
- what has helped them;
- what they would like more of;
- what they would like to change; and
- what they would introduce.

In addition to an audit with parents, it may be useful to understand how confident staff feel about working with parents. The SENCO can support the teacher with the Assess, Plan, Do, Review process, however, the teacher is responsible and accountable for the pupils in their class, and having conversations with parents may be intimidating. Day (2013) suggests that for an effective working relationship with parents, staff need to be able to:

- give information or advice;
- be flexible;
- be sensitive to the individual needs of the family; and
- have a good breadth of knowledge of both SEN and the system.

Therefore, as a SENCO you may want to identify answers to the following:

- Do staff have access to information?
- Do they have knowledge of SEN and the system?
- Would they benefit from either whole-school, departmental or individual additional support in this area? Strategies as suggested in Chapter 5, 'Leading and supporting colleagues', may help, for example pairing up teachers. However, SENCOs may need to target their time to demonstrate how to lead difficult conservations. It is worth noting that the SEND Code of Practice (DfE and DoH, 2015) suggests that this can be a sensitive area and may present a training need for staff.

Involving parents at a strategic level

It is also worth considering that your parents may be one of your best resources when you are considering making changes; perhaps you have identified a system you specifically want to improve. Speak to your parents. For example, for parents who have been through the Education, Health and Care needs assessment process, what worked well for them, and what would have helped? They might cite changes which are outside of your remit, but you can pass this on. Are there recurrent themes, indicating that there is something more systemic that you need to address?

Invite parents to consult on policy reviews, new processes and the school SEN information report. This allows parents to not only be part of the process, but also meet other parents.

Longer-term planning

Desforges and Abouchaar (2003) report that it takes three years to embed changes related to developing parental voice. This can be detailed within your SEN development plan. However, whilst there needs to be a consistent commitment to focusing on developing parental relationships, there also needs to be staff training and the development of resources. Ultimately, for those of you who have identified, through your SEN audit and/or development plan, that engagement with pupils and parents is a priority, use policy as your friend. Use it to drive forward change in your setting but implement this in a planned and strategic manner.

Systems of support across the school

Think about ways in which you can create specific avenues of support for parents. This might include:

- an informal drop in surgery for parents;
- a coffee morning for parents whose children have special educational needs. You might want to consider having a specific focus, for example fine motor skills or dyslexia; or
- making sure there is a system across the school which ensures parents are communicated with effectively. This is particularly important if additional work or activities are being suggested at home. Three teachers suggesting three different activities, plus a few recommendations from external agencies, and the expectation on home-learning can quickly become overwhelming.

Something to think about

Consider the information which is given to parents at the start of the process, when the school is considering whether the child may have additional needs.

Questions to think about regarding your processes:

- What information is given to parents regarding the process for identifying SEN in your school?
- How are next steps communicated?

- Who is their 'go to' person, and how do they know this?
- Is communication proactive or reactive?
- What is the process for ensuring parents are formally informed if special educational provision is being made?
- How do you signpost parents, for example to the local authority Information, Advice and Support Service?
- How do you support parents in navigating the school, and wider, system? Do you provide a jargon buster?

Translate

One of the key issues experienced by parents is the lack of transparency and confusing nature of the SEN system (Day, 2013). On your school website you must have:

- your SEN policy; and
- your SEN information report.

However, these documents are not always parent friendly. There is a balance here of ensuring that you have included all the relevant information, but you have also made it clear and accessible. It is particularly important to consider how transparent your systems are at school. Are parents aware of who they can contact and what the processes for supporting their child are?

To support access and understanding of the content in these key documents, consider:

- When it is time to review your SEN policy, create a working party of parents to review the document with a specific view to how clear and understandable it is.
- Create short versions of the SEN policy and SEN information report.
- Create a visual document illustrating the Assess, Plan, Do, Review process and how this happens in your school.
- Share an acronym sheet with parents. Include this on your website and when you send out information to parents (see Appendix).
- Review the accessibility of the language used in school documents, specifically those aimed at parents. Websites such as the Simplified Measure of Gobbledegook (SMOG) calculator can help you identify the level you are writing at. For example, according to the algorithm, this section of text is at post-graduate studies level.
- When working with external agencies, discuss with them how they intend to ensure that their report is accessible for pupils and parents. Ask them to create a one page overview. This can be a useful discussion tool for parents and a quick way of informing teachers of the outcome of the input.

93

Signpost

In addition to support at school, an important role of the SENCO is signposting parents to wider support. This can help build their networks and create further avenues of support. Signposting can be carried out in a number of ways:

- SEN notice board.
- SEN newsletter.
- School newsletter.
- Letters to parents.
- Information sheets at the start of the identification process.
- Create a quick information pack. The pack could contain quick guides to specific areas of SEN, networks or statutory processes. This may help demystify the SEN system. These could be made accessible on your website.

Consider the information which may help parents. You may wish to signpost to:

- the Local Offer;
- Parent Partnership;
- specific local charities; and
- specific local support groups.

Develop a robust key worker system

Central to developing good relationships is timely communication. For most SENCOs, given the earlier report challenges with time and workload, it would be impossible for them to be the key point of contact with parents. Equally, as the SEND Code of Practice (DfE and DoH, 2015) states, every teacher is a teacher of SEN and responsibility lies with the class or subject teacher. However, this can be problematic, particularly in secondary schools, as there are a number of teachers who are working, concurrently, with the child. A key worker system can help this, where children are assigned a key worker to whom they can go, and who parents can contact, in the first instance. In some cases, this is the form tutor, however a number of SENCOs I know have worked with teaching assistants taking on this role and they have reported that this can create a good dynamic, as well as expanding the SEN team.

Consider the nature of messages shared

A school I work with, every time they phone home, begins the conversation 'Hello it is X school, don't worry it is nothing to worry about'. It is natural for parents to feel anxious if they see a missed call or a message from school because, typically, no news is good news. This may be heightened for parents whose children have additional needs. Parents may feel stressed coming into the playground if, every time they do, they are approached by a member of staff with more bad news (Day, 2013). It is therefore no surprise that parents may start to avoid the playground.

Part of the keyworker's role could be to ensure that positive messages are sent home. These can include:

- sending texts home;
- emails specifically in relation to targets met or achievements;
- postcards;
- phone calls with good news; or
- post it notes with websites or key books to show you are mindful of their child.

Anticipate times when more support might be needed

When you are planning your SENCO year, think about the times of the year which may be stressful for families. This may include Christmas, and exam and transition periods to name but a few. There may also be activities, which the school views as enriching and exciting, which may cause anxiety for a family. For example, Christmas plays or annual school trips. Work with the family in advance to determine the support they need. However, take the lead from the parents and know when it is important to advocate on behalf of a parent for a child taking part, or indeed a child not taking part. Many of these points in the year can be anticipated, therefore try, in as far as is possible, to anticipate some of the concerns and start to plan for these, beginning with talking to the parents.

Family relationships: individual approaches

Parents as experts

Be clear with parents, and with staff, that you need and value the experience and skills that parents have to reach the very best outcomes for the children and young people. One of the SENCOs I worked with stated that 'teachers were the experts in education and parents were the experts in their children. It is not until the two come together that we can really begin to see progress'. Make sure that you foster an expectation across the school that the parent's view is vital and expected. The parent is truly the expert and may have developed over time a range of strategies that work, as well as knowledge of those which do not. Save yourself time by discussing the strategies with the parents. However, do not assume that the parents understand everything about their child's specific needs. Ensure that you work with the family and support them in their developing knowledge regarding their specific child's needs.

Identifying priorities

It may be that the pupil and parents have very different priorities to those held by the school. The school may be focused on a child meeting a particular learning outcome, whereas the parent may be more focused on trying to develop a calm bedtime. Ensure that the parent's aspirations are valued and incorporated into the plan. This may be a moment where the SENCO needs to advocate on behalf of the parents.

Tailoring communication

We live in a communication-rich environment with multiple ways of communicating with people, at various times. Due to the specific circumstances of parents, traditional methods of communicating with them, for example in face-to-face meetings or via letter, may not be convenient. Feedback from parents will provide you with a 'default' method of communicating, but it is worth checking in with parents to see if they prefer:

- email;
- letter;
- phone call; or
- text.

In terms of face-to-face communication, think about the times of meetings and how these suit parents. Parents may be working full time or may have younger children, both of which can make day time meetings challenging. Ask the parents what would work for them. Ensure that parents have plenty of notice for meetings, so they can arrange additional support if needed.

Think about the whole family

There are a number of factors which may impact on the parent's engagement with school. Factors may include, amongst others:

- further children with additional needs;
- children at different schools;
- younger children;
- lone parent families; and
- English as an additional language.

It is worth considering whether any of these factors may present a barrier for engagement with parents. However, it is also important to think about the whole family, in particular for children who may have more complex needs. Would the parents, or the siblings in the family, benefit from some additional support? This could be offering a drop-in mentoring session for the siblings, or signposting to local charities that offer support in this area.

Formal multi-agency meetings

Multi-agency meetings have the power to create impact. They often act as a gatekeeper to accessing additional support or creating a plan of action. However, imagine walking into a room full of strangers who wanted to talk about you and make plans for your career. Imagine that they held the power to give you the support you needed to move forward in the direction you want to go, or to take away the support which is helping you move forward. It is hard to overstate the impact formal meetings can have on parents. They are walking into a room, typically full of professionals, who are deciding on provision and outcomes for their children. As such, these meetings can feel intimidating and overwhelming. There are a few things you can do as a SENCO to make the situation easier for parents:

- Ask the parents when the best time for a meeting is. If they can't attend, can they phone in or Skype? If they can't attend, can you prepare something together beforehand so you can read out what they want to say.
- Set an agenda beforehand so that the parent knows exactly what is going to be discussed and in what order. This gives them time to think through what they want to say. If possible, co-produce the agenda together.
- If time allows, have a pre-meeting together. Find out what the parent is worried about. Is there anything that they want to say? Make sure you note what they want to communicate. If they are not able to in the meeting, you can act as a prompt or advocate for them. However, agree this in advance as a potential strategy.
- Think about your seating plan. Who would the parent be comfortable sitting next to? Consider sitting next to the parents or asking them where they would like to go.
- Make sure you introduce everybody on first name terms. So often I have sat in meetings where introductions have followed Dr Smith, Mrs Jones and 'Mum'. This is not to disregard the importance of the name 'Mum', but equality and informality can help put everyone at ease.
- Decide who is going to chair the meeting and who is going to take minutes. Make sure actions are reiterated at the end and attribute to those who are undertaking them.

- Ensure the parent has the opportunity to ask questions at the end of the meeting. If you think there were some aspects which were not clear, ask for clarification on their behalf.
- Consider a de-brief meeting with the parents a few days afterwards, to ensure that they are clear on next steps.

Specific circumstances: Education, Health and Care plans

It is worth considering, as a SENCO, the specific needs and challenges a family who are involved with the Education, Health and Care (EHC) plan process may experience, whether they are at the start of the process or on their tenth annual review. Specific feelings, concerns and/or anxieties may surface at specific times. It is also important to consider the tailored support parents may need when going through this process. Detailing the process of a need's assessment, with a view to moving forward to an EHC plan, is outside of the remit of this chapter, however, it is important to be familiar with the SEND Code of Practice (DfE and DoH, 2015) and keep returning to this when moving through this process.

In addition to this, you may want to signpost parents to various avenues of support, including:

- IPSEA www.ipsea.org.uk;
- Contact www.contact.org.uk;
- local Parent Partnership website;
- Council for Disabled Children www.councilfordisabledchildren.org.uk; and
- Special Needs Jungle www.specialneedsjungle.com.

It's not always going to go how you planned

Finally, it is worth remembering that despite the best planning, working with children, young people and families means the changes you make will not always go to plan. As a SENCO, it is important to be not only resilient, but also reflective. Often, I am asked by SENCOs, 'but what do we do if the pupil/parent won't or can't engage with us?' I always answer with a question, 'what options do you have? You can keep going trying different solutions, or you can give up, which of these routes is going to help the child?' As such, it is important to look backwards as well as looking forwards.

- Remind yourself of when things have worked. Focus on the positive.
- When things have not worked, ask what might help next time.

- If relationships have broken down, seek a member of staff who can act as an intermediary. This is where the key worker system can be particularly effective.
- Go back to the beginning, remind everyone of your intended outcomes for the child, and the purpose of what you are doing.
- Gather support from your networks. The next chapter will look at how to manage challenges and developing your network is part of this. Your network will support you in unpicking, understanding and reflecting on situations, with a problem solving focus.

In summary

This chapter has provided an overview of the policy context for focusing on and developing relationships with pupils and parents in school. However, whilst the benefits to the collective and the individual have been explored, it is noted that there may be barriers which impact on the development of pupil–parental engagement in your school. The chapter may have provided more questions than answers, however, it is important that as a SENCO you reflect on your own school context and the specific needs of pupils and parents to further develop relationships and collaboration. As a reminder, this chapter is designed to act as a tool box from which you can draw a few ideas, try out and then return to. Finally, it is important to identify good practice in your school where pupil and parental engagement is considered a strength. This is the springboard from which you can develop further.

References

Children and Families Act 2014, ch. 6. Available at: www.legislation.gov.uk/ukpga/2014/6/pdfs/ukpga_20140006_en.pdf (Accessed 1st August 2014).

Day, S. (2013) '"Terms of engagement" not "hard to reach parents"', *Educational Psychology in Practice*, 29 (1), pp. 36–53.

Department for Children, Schools and Families (DCFS). (2009) *The lamb inquiry: Special educational needs and parental confidence*. Available at: webarchive.nationalarchives.gov.uk/20130401151715/www.education.gov.uk/publications/eOrderingDownload/01143-2009DOM-EN.pdf (Accessed 2nd February 2013).

Department for Education (DfE). (2012) *Support and aspiration: A new approach to special educational needs and disability*. Available at: www.gov.uk/government/uploads/system/uploads/attachment_data/file/198141/Support_and_Aspiration_Green-Paper-SEN.pdf (Accessed 15th March 2015).

Department for Education (DfE) and Department of Health (DoH). (2015) *Special educational needs and disability Code of Practice: 0–25 years.* Available at: www.gov.uk/government/uploads/system/uploads/attachment_data/file/398815/SEND_Code_of_Practice_January_2015.pdf (Accessed 1st February 2015).

Department of Education and Science (DES). (1978) *Special educational needs: Report of the committee of enquiry into the education of handicapped children and young people.* Available at: www.educationengland.org.uk/documents/warnock/warnock1978.html (Accessed 30th September 2014).

Desforges, C. and Abouchaar, A. (2003) *The impact of parental involvement, parental support and family education on pupil achievement and adjustment: A literature review.* Available at: www.nationalnumeracy.org.uk/sites/default/files/the_impact_of_parental_involvement.pdf (Accessed 3rd January 2019).

Edwards, S. (2016) *The SENCO survival guide: The nuts and bolts of everything you need to know.* London: Routledge.

Flutter, J. (2007) 'Teacher development and pupil voice', *Curriculum Journal*, 18 (3), pp. 343–354.

Heitin, R.C. (2013) 'Advocating for children and their families within the school system: Reflections of a long-time special education advocate', *Odyssey: New Directions in Deaf Education*, 14, pp. 44–47.

Hornby, G. and Lafaele, R. (2011) 'Barriers to parental involvement in education: An explanatory model', *Educational Review*, 63 (1), pp. 37–52.

Lauchlan, F. and Greig, S. (2015) 'Educational inclusion in England: Origins, perspectives and current directions', *Support for Learning*, 30 (1), pp. 69–82.

Marsh, H. (2012) 'Relationships for learning: Using pupil voice to define teacher-pupil relationships that enhance pupil engagement', *Management in Education*, 26 (3), pp. 161–163.

NASEN. (2015) *The SEND Code of Practice: 0–25 years. A quick guide to the SEND Code of Practice: 0–25 years (2014) and its implications for schools and settings.* Available at: file:///C:/Users/Helen/Downloads/the_send_code_of_practice_0_to_25_years_-_mini_guide%20(1).pdf (Accessed 10th June 2017).

Norwich, B. (2017) 'The future of inclusive education in England: Some lessons from current experiences of special educational needs', *Reach*, 30 (1), pp. 4–21.

Norwich, B. and Kelly, N. (2006) 'Evaluating children's participation in SEN procedures: Lessons for educational psychologists', *Educational Psychology in Practice*, 22 (3), pp. 255–271.

United Nations. (1989) *United Nations Convention on the Rights of the Child.* Available at: http://353ld710iigr2n4po7k4kgvv-wpengine.netdna-ssl.com/wp-content/uploads/2010/05/UNCRC_PRESS200910web.pdf (Accessed 3rd October 2016).

Whitty, G. and Wisby, E. (2007) 'Whose voice? An exploration of the current policy interest in pupil involvement in school decision-making', *International Studies in Sociology of Education*, 17 (3), p. 303.

Managing your role
Challenges and opportunities

The previous chapters have explored the SENCO role, as it is stated in policy, and have asked you to consider how this relates to your role within school, as well as how, as a leader, advisor and advocate, you can strategically develop SEN and inclusive provision in your school. However, whether you are a new or experienced SENCO, having thought about your current SENCO role and the activities you spend most of your time doing, as well as the tasks and priorities you have identified that you would like to focus on, you might immediately be thinking about the potential challenges and barriers which may impact on you being able to successfully move forward. There may be a host of reasons as to why you currently do not feel able to conduct your role as you would ideally envisage. Issues such as a lack of time to undertake the role, a potential lack of seniority to facilitate change, or feelings of being overwhelmed with the sheer volume of work are reasons often cited by SENCOs as barriers to them effectively facilitating their role (Szwed, 2007a; Curran et al., 2018).

The purpose of this chapter is to explore these issues, with a view to supporting SENCO well-being. However, there will be a specific problem-solving focus on what you can do to facilitate your role at both a micro and macro level. The chapter will consider how shaping your role can help with time management, as well as looking at ways in which you can develop a SEN team, either formally or informally, to help increase not only your support network, but also your capacity. Finally, the chapter will conclude by looking at the steps you can take to protect and support yourself in your role, particularly if you are undertaking the National Award for SEN Coordination (NA SENCO).

In summary, this chapter focuses on how to manage challenges associated with the SENCO role, including:

- time and workload;
- resources;
- it's not just you: grow your networks; and
- managing the National Award for SEN Coordination.

Time and workload

When the SENCO role was introduced, it quickly became apparent that a lack of time to execute the responsibilities of the role was a limiting factor, with Garner describing this as a 'crucial concern' (1996, p. 180). This can be attributed to the increase in bureaucracy for the person appointed, due to the wide range of duties and responsibilities (Derrington, 1997). It was proposed that the introduction of the 2001 Code (DfES, 2001) would reduce the level of paperwork SENCOs were having to manage (Bowers et al., 1998). However, this aim was not realised, and the 2001 Code (DfES, 2001) continued to place an unnecessary burden on SENCOs (Lingard, 2001). Lingard stated that, in particular, too much time was spent focused on the creation of Individual Education Plans (IEPs) for children with SEN. While these were not a requirement of the 2001 Code, Lingard argues that there was an understanding that Ofsted required these, hence their adoption by SENCOs and schools.

Certainly, Cowne's (2005) work found that time to execute the role was a key concern for many SENCOs, with Szwed (2007a) stating that too many SENCOs were overwhelmed by the role, partly due to the diverse nature of it but, also, the related bureaucracy. This led, in part, to a lack of time to execute the role (Rosen-Webb, 2011; Qureshi, 2014). School leaders were not investing adequately, in terms of time or money, in the role of the SENCO to address such issues (Layton, 2005). This was particularly true for primary SENCOs (Szwed, 2007b), which again suggests that the role is greater than one person and should encompass a team (Pearson and Ralph, 2007; Szwed, 2007c).

The 2001 Code (DfES, 2001), and the revised SEND Code of Practice (DfE and DoH, 2015), do not stipulate how much time is necessary for the SENCO to fulfil their duties. As Cowne (2005) states, context is imperative and, therefore, this has led to discrepancies in practice. However, Cowne concedes that SENCOs often have inadequate non-contact time to fulfil their responsibilities. Recent research has echoed this, with 70% of SENCOs stating that they do not have enough time to fulfil the role, with 95% of SENCOs believing that they should have protected time (Curran et al., 2018). Overlapping roles and shifting priorities can also impact on the time that a SENCO has to dedicate to the role (Derrington, 1997; Bowers et al., 1998; Cole, 2005; Mackenzie, 2007; Szwed, 2007a; Curran et al., 2018). It could be argued that this specific barrier also impacts on the strategic nature of the role.

Time to undertake the SENCO role, in addition to the high levels of bureaucracy associated with it, can lead to feelings of being overburdened. In such situations it is understandable that SENCOs can feel powerless to bring about change. It could be argued that in times of budget cuts it is even more challenging for SENCOs to try and secure the non-contact time they need to complete the role. So, what can you do?

Know your role

As stated above, it is important that you know what you should be doing as a SENCO. However, it is also important that you know what you should not be doing. There needs to be clear parameters around your role to ensure that you are focusing on the areas which need to be focused on, but equally, your attention is not being diverted to tasks which should not come under your remit (refer back to the earlier chapters related to the SENCO role – Chapter 2, 'The SENCO role in policy and practice' and Chapter 5, 'Leading and Supporting Colleagues').

Inform colleagues about the SENCO role and the time you need

It could be argued that one of the key issues with the SENCO role is how the role is understood by colleagues, particularly by senior leaders. You need to think about how to communicate this to all those you work with, including staff and parents. By ensuring that your colleagues understand your role, it will not only help to raise its profile, but it will also help your colleagues understand where they fit into the system for supporting children with SEN.

A recent survey of over 1900 SENCOs found that less than half of SENCOs (46%) felt that their role was understood by senior leaders in their schools, and only 27% of SENCOs felt that colleagues in their school understood their role, with one SENCO stating, 'I don't think any of the senior leadership team realise how big a job the SENCO is … Splitting yourself into a million pieces (the biggest being a classroom full-time class teacher) and manage SEN is extremely hard' (Curran et al., 2018). Therefore, it is imperative that you are clear with senior leaders and governors not only regarding the nature of the role, but the time you need to carry it out. Things you can do:

- Share with your senior leadership team, your head teacher and the governing body the National SENCO Workload Survey – *It's about time: The impact of SENCO workload on the professional and the school* (Curran et al., 2018).
- Also share the guidance for SENCO time allocation by school size and cohort (see Appendix 7.1). This data was developed from the National SENCO Workload Survey and reflects the amount of time SENCOs believe they need to effectively undertake the role.
- Ensure that you have a clear job description.

- With the time that you have, be clear as to what this means that you can and can't do, and what the impact of this means for the children and school. The National SENCO Workload Survey found that over 50% of all respondents were working at least an extra 9 hours or more per week on SENCO related tasks, in addition to any allocated SENCO time. For secondary school SENCOs, the number increased to nearly three-quarters (71%). This is not sustainable. School leaders need to understand the true picture of the role and this means being clear as to what you can realistically achieve in the time that you have been allocated.

- If you feel that you do not have enough time, make a request. Outline what your current time allows you to do, and what the additional time will enable you to achieve, noting the potential wider impact on children and staff. However, if you feel that it is unlikely that you will be able to access additional, regular SENCO time, consider identifying specific times in the year when you will need additional time.

Ideas in action

Jo had been SENCO for six months. During this time, she had got to grips with the basics of the role but was not sure how to share with colleagues and parents what she did. At the time, Jo felt that she had been increasingly 'firefighting', in particular she was frustrated with the lack of understanding of how long things took, for example submitting a request for a need's assessment.

Jo began by meeting with her SEN governor. They decided that Jo would come to a governing body meeting and present a brief overview of her role. They felt that this would help not only governors, but also the head teacher and SLT who attended, understand her role more.

Jo also then developed a crib sheet for teachers, which outlined their role and responsibilities, and hers, and how the two interrelated. She emphasised the 'Co-ordinator' aspects of the role, as well as highlighting the responsibilities within the SEND Code of Practice (DfE and DoH, 2015), in particular the 'advising' element. This crib sheet was introduced at the start of a staff meeting, as a way in which everyone could be clear regarding their responsibilities.

Mindful that some staff may feel concerned about their responsibilities, Jo carried out a quick audit of training, skills and areas for skill development. Additional training sessions were then planned to address gaps in skills which had been identified (see Chapter 5, 'Leading and Supporting Colleagues').

Plan your SENCO year

It may be difficult for you to secure additional time for your SENCO role. However, it is likely that there will be times within the year when you can predict that it will be particularly busy. These may include:

- End and/or beginning of the academic year due to transition for both children and parents.
- Christmas and other periods of change.
- Exams – including access arrangements.
- Education, Health and Care (EHC) plan reviews.

If you are already feeling that you do not have enough time to complete your role, it may be useful to think about times of the year when you are going to need extra administrative support or additional time. Presenting a case for additional time, due to an increase in demands, may help you alleviate these pressure points. Consider the variety of support which might help you. For example, during EHC plan review time, would additional administrative support be helpful?

Have a contingency plan

The SENCO role is unpredictable. The best laid plans can swiftly change if an emergency crops up. As such it is important, in terms of your time, to have a contingency plan. It is not sustainable for you to manage all of your roles, and deal with an emergency at the same time; there needs to be a contingency plan in place for either additional time or additional personnel at times of unexpected emergencies. This may be in the form of having an arrangement in place for someone who can cover your class at short notice, permission to miss staff meetings at particular pinch points in the year or emergency admin cover.

Something to think about

Think about the last time an emergency or unexpected situation arose at school which needed your direct input and attention.

How did you manage this?

What would have helped you manage the situation more effectively?

Know the law

In the previous chapters we have referred to the SEND Code of Practice (DfE and DoH, 2015) and used the guidance as the starting point to un-pick the role of the SENCO, and the role of others, in relation to everyday practice in school. However, the SEND Code of Practice is the statutory guidance for all those who work with children and young people with SEN. As such, it is also the 'go to' guide for SENCOs in terms of wider processes and responsibilities of others. In short, the SEND Code of Practice (DfE and DoH, 2015) which applies to England, is for:

- head teachers and principals;
- governing bodies;
- school and college staff;
- SENCOs;
- early education providers;
- local authorities; and
- health and social services staff.

This statutory code contains:

- details of legal requirements that you must follow without exception; and
- statutory guidance that you must follow, by law, unless there's a good reason not to.

Therefore, whilst it is important to know your role and the role of others within school, it is imperative to refer to the SEND Code of Practice (DfE and DoH, 2015) and to be clear as to what you should be doing, and what is actually the remit of others.

It is also worth noting the language used within the SEND Code of Practice. For example, did you know: 'In this Code of Practice, where the text uses the word 'must' it refers to a statutory requirement under primary legislation, regulations or case law' (DfE and DoH, 2015, p. 12).

The following example looks at the process of requesting a needs assessment for a child or young person who may require an Education, Health and Care plan. One of the key issues I have heard over the years from SENCOs are the challenges that they experience when they are trying to move toward a need's assessment. SENCOs have reported that they have to provide reams of evidence, they need to engage the services of external agencies, or they must have an educational psychology report before they can make the request. A key issue for SENCOs is the amount of time it takes to complete the required paperwork. However, when the legislation and related guidance is considered, it states:

> A local authority must conduct an assessment of education, health and care needs when it considers that it may be necessary for special educational provision to be made for the child or young person in accordance with an EHC plan.
>
> (DfE and DoH, 2015, p. 142)

The 2014 Children and Families Act states:

> The local authority must secure an EHC needs assessment for the child or young person if, after having regard to any views expressed and evidence submitted under subsection (7), the authority is of the opinion that –
>
> (a) the child or young person has or may have special educational needs, and
> (b) it may be necessary for special educational provision to be made for the child or young person in accordance with an EHC plan.

In terms of submitting evidence, the SEND Code of Practice (DfE and DoH, 2015) states that when the LA is considering whether to proceed with a need's assessment, they should consider a range of evidence and 'should pay particular attention to':

- evidence of the child or young person's academic attainment (or developmental milestones in younger children) and rate of progress;
- information about the nature, extent and context of the child or young person's SEN;
- evidence of the action already being taken by the early year's provider, school or post-16 institution to meet the child or young person's SEN;
- evidence that where progress has been made, it has only been as the result of much additional intervention and support over and above that which is usually provided;
- evidence of the child or young person's physical, emotional and social development and health needs, drawing on relevant evidence from clinicians and other health professionals and what has been done to meet these by other agencies; and
- where a young person is aged over 18, the local authority must consider whether the young person requires additional time, in comparison to the majority of others of the same age who do not have special educational needs, to complete their education or training. Remaining in formal education or training should help young people to achieve education and training outcomes, building on what they have learned before and preparing them for adult life.

(DfE and DoH, 2015, pp. 145–146)

It is notable that the LA 'may develop criteria as guidelines to help them decide when it is necessary to carry out an EHC needs assessment and must be prepared to depart from those criteria where there is a compelling reason to do so' (DfE and DoH, 2015,

p. 146). However, no specific forms or particular types of evidence are stipulated in the SEND Code of Practice as a requirement for a needs assessment request. Therefore, this suggests that it is helpful to develop a link with your LA Officer to determine exactly what is required when submitting a request for a needs assessment, yet, at the same time, being aware of the law and the SEND Code of Practice, which does not stipulate any specific processes or evidence. This is one example where SENCO workload may have increased due to undertaking activities, or following processes, which are not actually required.

Something to think about

One of the challenges for a SENCO is paperwork. Consider what is necessary and what is required. This may be true of the annual review requirements.

Have a read of Chapter 9, pages 195 onwards, of the SEND Code of Practice (DfE and DoH, 2015). This discusses the processes for EHCP annual reviews. Whilst the school must prepare and send a report of the meeting within two weeks, there is no legal requirement to comply with LA specific paperwork. For SENCOs who have pupils from varying LAs, it could be a timesaver not to fill out LA-specific paperwork every time. However, it is also important to maintain and develop professional relationships. Is this something you could raise with your Local Authority Officer?

Develop your processes

A key challenge associated with the SENCO role is the lack of magic wands which are given out on appointment to the role! You may have found that as soon as you took on the role, gone were the days of being able to walk down the corridor without someone asking you a question. You may find that you are repeatedly stopped and asked for advice, or even asked 'what are you going to do about X?' Naturally, this is part of the role and relates to the SEND Code of Practice (DfE and DoH, 2015), which states that SENCOs will be overseeing the day-to-day operation of the SEN policy, coordinating provision for children and advising teachers. However, an ad hoc approach to sharing information is not productive and does not help teachers in retaining overall responsibility for children with SEN. Earlier in the book we explored the benefits of developing an 'in house' referral system, and how this can help develop the strategic side of the role, support teachers with how they see their role within the Assess, Plan, Do, Review system, and provide opportunities for professional develop. Additionally, such a system can also support you in managing and balancing your role. Such a process can help you:

- prioritise your time;
- track and monitor impact; and
- ensure that you are remaining within the 'coordinator' side of the role.

Ideas in action

Simon was increasingly frustrated by the number of 'ad hoc' conversations he was having with teachers regarding concerns they had about children. He felt concerned that he may miss something due to the important nature of the conversations. He was also concerned that teachers felt they had then 'passed on' the issue to him, and as such they were not taking on board their role as a teacher.

Having spoken to his SENCO network, Simon decided to trial the introduction of a 'concern referral sheet'. If a teacher had concerns about a particular child they had to complete the referral form. The form asked for detail regarding:

- the nature of the concern;
- supporting evidence;
- what approaches and strategies they had already tried to help support the child;
- what had and hadn't worked; and
- whether they had spoken to the parents.

Once Simon had trialled the form with a colleague, he made a few changes, including prompts regarding 'what have you tried?', then introduced the form at a staff meeting. Simon is still stopped in the corridor now but instead of teachers asking him 'what can you do?', he is asking teachers 'have you completed a referral form?'. He is able to review each form, monitor on-going concerns, and prioritise his response.

Resources

It is unequivocal that the current educational landscape is set against a backdrop of economic austerity, which is having a significant impact on schools; Pearson and colleagues (2015) predicted that resources would decrease as a direct result of the SEND reforms. This means that if you have access to financial resources as part of your SENCO role, you may find that these are rapidly reducing and you are having to do more with less. Equally you may find that you are in a position of having to make tough choices regarding provision and prioritising access to resources. However, unlike many other roles, such as therapists or counsellors, SENCOs do not typically have access to supervision. This means that SENCOs can be making decisions in isolation, without the benefit of input from others. This can be particularly challenging as often it is useful to talk out your ideas. On the other hand, SENCOs may find that they are trying to fill the gap left by a lack of resources, often at personal cost, because they try to fill the gap themselves.

Therefore, there are three points to consider:

1) Do we currently provide value for money in terms of provision?
2) How can you access services through means which you may not have considered before?
3) How can you protect yourself from trying to fill the gap?

It is important to review not only the impact additional provision has in your school, but also the value for money it provides. One of the key tools you can use to consider this is provision mapping. The SEND Code of Practice states that, 'Provision maps are an efficient way of showing all the provision that the school makes which is additional to and different from that which is offered through the school's curriculum' (DfE and DoH, 2015, p. 105). It also adds that provision maps can be used to monitor impact, identify patterns of need and interventions which are effective, as well as 'removing those which are less so' (DfE and DoH, 2015, p. 106). Therefore, provision maps can be used as a tool through which you can make judgements regarding the allocation of your SEN budget.

Ideas in action

The SEND Code of Practice (DfE and DoH, 2015) refers to further provision mapping guidance – find this in the SEND Code of Practice reference list.

You can also find out more about provision mapping through nasen and the SEND Gateway.

In response to the second point listed above, it is time to get creative. The starting point needs to be your local authority's Local Offer. This should detail the support which can be expected for children with additional needs in your locality. However, you may also want to look at charities and other organisations which may provide the services you require.

Economies of scale

One of the potential benefits of working in a cluster of schools is that you have the benefit of economies of scale. As such, consider whether you can make more use of your networks to access resources, either through collectively buying in support services or through shared training. Are there training sessions which the SENCOs in the cluster can attend, which can then be disseminated to the school?

Whilst there are many ways in which you can get creative when trying to access resources, it is imperative that you protect yourself. Research has shown that SENCOs are working over and above their allocated hours to 'get the job done' (Curran et al., 2018). In addition to this, SENCOs are seeking to replicate services which perhaps they used to externally access, particularly in relation to social, emotional and mental health support. Prior to developing any further support, it is important to consider how feasible and, ultimately, sustainable it is for the SENCO to be offering practical intervention directly to children. It is also important to consider the wider impact undertaking additional work may bring, for example will it impact on the strategic development of your role, or will it potentially give a false view of the capacity of the SENCO role?

It's not just you: grow your networks

Shortly after the 1994 Code (DfE, 1994) was introduced, Bowers et al. (1998) noted that the role was likely to have a personal impact on the professional undertaking it, with Mackenzie later describing the post as 'enormously demanding' (2007, p. 212). Derrington (1997) suggested that a large number of SENCOs undertook a significant amount of out of hours work to fulfil their duties. In addition to the complex nature of the role, which can cause stress (Rosen-Webb, 2011), the role has been described as unmanageable (Mackenzie, 2007). While head teachers can be sources of support (Mackenzie, 2007), the nature of the role can leave SENCOs vulnerable to becoming over-burdened (Szwed, 2007c). This perhaps explains, in part, why the role of the SENCO has traditionally had a high turnover (Pearson, 2008).

Just the one SENCO?

Hallett and Hallett (2010) suggest that it is the breadth of role, as portrayed by Kearns (2005), which highlights the need for the responsibilities to be fulfilled by more than one person. Mackenzie (2007), in agreement with Hallett and Hallett, suggests that the SENCO was never intended to be the sole person responsible for SEND. Certainly, Szwed (2007c) would argue that the term SENCO should have a plurality. However, this is not echoed in policy; the statutory requirement echoed in the National Award for SEN Coordination Learning Outcomes (NCTL, 2014) is to have one person overseeing SEN in schools (DfES, 2001; DfE and DoH, 2015), and the SEND Code of Practice (DfE and DoH, 2015) refers to the SENCO in a singular sense. It is, however, worth thinking about how you can develop your SENCO team, either formally or informally.

- Administrative support – either regular, planned or ad hoc. See section above re colleagues understanding your role.
- Assistant or deputy SENCO – are there any teachers in your school who are looking to move into the role of the SENCO? There is the possibility here to develop the role of an assistant or deputy SENCO, to allow the teacher in question to develop their skills and knowledge, and gain experience in this area, whilst also providing much needed support to you.
- SEN team – formal and informal. It can be hugely supportive to work within a SEN team, which may consist of an assistant or deputy SENCO, or teaching assistants and support staff. Not only can this support you professionally, but this can have an impact on the development of inclusive practice in your school. Consider ways in which you can develop a team ethos, from the way in which you communicate, to where you are based and how accessible you are. You may not have a 'direct' team, but when you begin to consider the people who are working with children with SEN in your school, you may realise the team is bigger than it first appears! For your own benefit, seek ways in which to develop your team.
- Consider the role of the SEN governor – it is important to consider what the role of the SEN governor is, but also to think about how they can support you in the execution of your role.
  - Find out where their skills lie and what their experience is. How can this help you in the execution of your role?
  - Meet regularly with your SEN governor but ensure that you have an agenda for the meeting and set a time frame.
  - Be clear as to how the SEN governor can support you. How can they be your champion? If you haven't been to a governors meeting to inform them of your role and the National Award for SEN Coordination, is this something that the SEN governor can do on your behalf?
  - Can they support you in accessing additional time, either related to the SENCO role or competing the NA SENCO?

o I advise my SENCOs that they can always send their assignments to their SEN governor to proof read – it also means that the SEN governor is developing their own knowledge of SEN at the same time!

Ideas in action

One SENCO I worked with worked in a large secondary school and had concerns that she was the 'only' person on her team. She was also worried about how to create effective links with parents when there was just the one of her! However, in addition to her role as SENCO, she was responsible for the deployment of teaching assistants. She decided to focus on developing her team of teaching assistants. She did this through:

- Appointing teaching assistants as key workers for specific children, who would act as a key point of contact for families.
- Creating a base for everyone. She opened up her office so the teaching assistants could come and speak to her, or each other, at any point.
- Creating meeting times, notice boards and other ways which illustrated that the teaching assistants were part of the team.
- Sending notifications to staff to illustrate who each key worker was.
- Ensuring all support staff were involved in any training opportunities.

Developing SENCO networks

SENCOs have often reported feelings of isolation. Typically, there is one SENCO in a school, particularly if you work in a smaller secondary or a primary school. As such, it can feel as if you are somewhat set apart from your colleagues as no one is conducting a role similar to yours. Therefore, it is extremely important that you think about how you are going to develop the networks around you. Having just considered how you can do this in school, it is also important to think about the networks you can develop outside of school. These may include:

- Support from neighbouring schools.
- Your local SENCO clusters.
- Support from across your multi-academy trust.
- Support from colleagues on the NA SENCO.
- Online support, such as Facebook forums or twitter. There are a number of 'chats' which take place weekly which often look at various topics.
- Support from organisations, such as Whole School SEND and nasen.

Sources of support

- Look out for hashtags #sencochat and #senexchange for weekly chats around various topics related to SEN.
- SEND Gateway.
- SENCO forum.
- nasen.
- Whole School SEND – find out who your local representative is.
- Consider the SENCOs you are already working with or have links with. Can you create a group of support? For example, sharing resources, CPD, or having someone else you can talk through ideas with.

Managing the National Award for SEN Coordination

A work–life balance is something that most teachers dream of. It could be argued that for SENCOs, this dream is even more elusive. However, it is imperative to look after your own well-being. One of the key challenges a new SENCO may experience, which will impact on work–life balance, is the requirement to undertake the NA SENCO. This places an additional requirement on SENCOs as they need to pass 60 credits at Masters level, which typically involves assignment writing of sorts.

Perhaps one of the key challenges a new SENCO may experience is the combination of undertaking a new, complex role, whilst also having to begin Masters level study. For some SENCOs, the challenge can be compounded because they may not have studied for some time, which can be daunting. Having taught on the NA SENCO for some years, I, together with my students, have drawn together a list of ideas which may help you as you start the NA SENCO.

Think about when to start

SENCOs who are new to the post, from 1st September 2009, have three years to gain the award. Typically, the majority of courses are a year to a year and a half in length. There are also a number of courses on offer, many of which offer differing start dates. As a new or aspiring SENCO, think about when you want to start the course, noting that you will need to have completed within three years. There are pros and cons to each:

- As an aspiring SENCO, undertaking the NA SENCO before you secure a post as a SENCO can enable you to access support from your school SENCO. You may not have the additional pressures of a 'full' SENCO role and, therefore, this may lessen the pressure. Often, schools who are succession planning, or seeking to create an additional SENCO role, adopt this approach. However, completing some elements whilst not in the role may be challenging.

- As a new SENCO who has recently secured a post, you may find that meeting with teachers who are in a similar position can be supportive and helpful. You will have accessible support, from both your tutors and other SENCOs, as you begin this exciting role. You can bring queries and questions to your sessions and begin to develop networks early on to support you and your colleagues. In my experience this tends to be the typical route SENCOs take. It does mean that you are beginning a new role at the same time as undertaking study, which can bring additional pressures, however the benefits are being able to immediately access support as soon as you start the role.
- As a new SENCO you may decide to wait a year before you start the award to allow yourself to settle into the role and to get to grips with one new thing at a time. This can mean that you are not overwhelmed with a new job and a new course at the same time. The downside is that you will not be able to access wider support immediately, and you may find that you would have done things differently if you had started the course earlier. You will also have less time to complete the qualification in order to meet the 2009 SENCO regulations. If you choose this route it would be important to consider other avenues of support which you can access in the first year, for example from within your multi-academy trust or from the local authority.

From a tutor's perspective it is always exciting to have a mixed group of SENCOs as it means there are varying experiences, attitudes and skills, which always makes for an interesting discussion.

Think about what mode of study will suit you

There will be a number of factors which will influence your decision as to where you decide to study. This may be returning to your previous university, using your local provider, or you may decide that online learning is best for you. Find out what is on offer locally and nationally. Make links with the course tutor and find out when the sessions are held, what the course requirements are and what support the course offers. There are pros and cons of each. Online study can give you the flexibility that you may need, and may be cheaper. However, face-to-face sessions give you the opportunity to meet other SENCOs, network and may also help keep the role prominent in school, especially if sessions are during the day. This can highlight the importance of the qualification, yet there may be additional costs to cover if you need to be out of school. It is worth exploring and talking to other SENCOs to find out their experience, both locally and through national networks.

Study tips

The majority of my students are returning to study after a break, often of many years. This can be very daunting. Furthermore, the additional challenge is that you are likely to be undertaking the NA SENCO at a time when you have a multitude of work and home commitments. Over the years I have worked with students to explore the various ways in which they can try and integrate studying into their lives, while managing all of the other, competing, priorities. The following are ideas we have developed:

- Get going as soon as possible. This is the advice I always give yet tend to ignore myself! The sooner you can get going with the academic reading, or any of the tasks associated with the course, the better.
- If you are someone who works well with a deadline, set yourself one which has some sort of external validation, e.g. tell your tutor when you will be sending them some work to review, or share a date with a colleague or family member as to when you will share with them a draft of your assignment.
- Know when you work best – set yourself up for success. We all have working patterns that work for us, either due to the times of day we have available, or how we feel at particular points in the day. Over the years I have come to realise that I am no good working in the evening, despite telling myself that 'I will get that report written tonight' or 'I will mark three assignments before I go to bed'. It doesn't happen and I then feel like I have failed. I am, however, an early riser and love the peace of the morning. Therefore, I capitalise on this. At times when I need to carry out extra work, I get up one hour earlier each day and this is protected time for whatever deadline I am working on.
- Protect the time. There is no end point to the SENCO role. As soon as you tick a job off your list, another is added. You need to protect your time and make sure that, if you have allocated an afternoon to work on an assignment, you do not let other activities impinge on this.
- To this end, think about where is best to work. Working on your assignment at school may be problematic, as you will still be available to staff and pupils. Make arrangements to work at home or at the library. If working at home is not feasible, think about other areas you can access where you can be undisturbed and away from distractions. This could be a university library, local library or a coffee shop.
- Read or write anything, however little. If you set aside an afternoon, but only end up with half an hour, do not discount it as 'not enough time'. Read one article or write one paragraph. Use any small amount of time that you have.
- Use the support network you have. Do you know of SENCOs who have completed the NA SENCO? If so, make links with them.

- Keep in touch. Your tutors and the NA SENCO provider are there to help you. They want you to pass and to do well. If there are any factors which are impacting on your ability to complete the course, let them know. Find out what other support systems might be in place to support you.
- With my students we set up virtual study groups, where students who are studying similar areas can share ideas, resources and key readings via email. This is something you can arrange yourself. Find out who is looking at the same area as you, either on the course or in your locality, and link up.

It is also worth remembering that it is not the SENCO's responsibility to make sure that they have the NA SENCO qualification. Whilst the NA SENCO is a mandatory award for all SENCOs new to the post (DfE and DoH, 2015), which must be achieved within three years of the SENCO being appointed, it is the responsibility of the governing bodies of maintained mainstream schools and the proprietors of mainstream academy schools (including free schools) that must ensure that there is a qualified teacher designated as SENCO. As such, it is important that your school, your SLT and your governing body are aware of the requirements of the course and the additional work which this may bring. In the past I have sent information to head teachers about workload in relation to this aspect. SENCOs have also managed to successfully negotiate additional time to ensure that they are able to meet the demands of the course.

In addition to this, there are some study tips which may help you:

- Devise a system for recording your reading immediately.
- Plan your work. Spending time on a thorough and detailed plan will pay dividends in the future when it comes to writing up your assignments. Plan under subheadings, and then plan each paragraph within this section. To develop your plan, you will need to read, but there comes a point when you then need to write!
- Reward yourself!
- Set your own targets, as you would for the children you support, and break it down. What are your steps to success? Are you aiming to write 600 words a week? Or read one article a week?
- Are there any moments which you could use to undertake a little more reading? I have been known to take journal articles with me to hospital appointments and whilst waiting for swimming lessons to finish!
- Make sure someone proof reads your assignment. This can be a colleague or your SEN governor – a good example of how you can covertly provide CPD for a colleague!
- Make sure you have down time.

Finally, this is for a short time only. You can do this! I have worked with over 350 SENCOs, many of whom, when they start the course, are greatly concerned about how they will fit it in. It is a challenge, but it can be done. Try and get the most out of it.

In summary

The SENCO role is hugely rewarding; in your role you have the potential to positively impact the lives of children and families in the long term. However, it is clear that the role comes with a number of challenges, one of the key challenges being that it is not only the breadth of the role, but how to manage the role, without protected time. In addition to this, it is clear that SENCOs are working over and above to try and meet the demands of the role (Curran et al., 2018), often to the detriment of their personal well-being. This chapter has sought to explore some of the most frequently reported challenges associated with the role, namely a lack of time, a lack of resources and, for those new to the role, the need to undertake an additional qualification at an already busy time. As a SENCO, it is important to consider how you can try and manage the demands of the role whilst protecting your well-being.

Appendix 7.1

Guidance for SENCO time allocation by school size and cohort

The recommendations in the tables below are drawn from respondents who identified as mainstream SENCOs working in a local authority maintained school, academy, multi-academy trust, or free school. Primary SENCO data was drawn from those SENCOs who identified as working in a first, infant, junior or primary school setting; secondary SENCOs were identified as working in a secondary, middle or upper school setting.

The guidance is based on data from the question 'how much time in total do you think you would need each week to be able to complete the demands of your SENCO role effectively?'

The data has been formulated through averaging the responses from SENCOs by different setting type, school size and percentage of SEN support. The data was also reviewed by geographical area (urban, rural and coastal), however the responses did not show significant enough variation to be distinguished into their own categories.

The greatest number of responses were from SENCOs in urban settings (68%), followed by rural (27%).

This data was also reviewed by number of EHCPs in the setting. Regardless of setting or SEN support percentage, there was a clear trend that the greater the number of EHCPs, the greater the demand of a SENCO's time. As such, further advice and guidance has been provided to enable SENCOs and head teachers to decide on a precise time allocation bespoke to each setting, including consideration of other factors identified through the data which also require more of a SENCO's time. These include:

- further qualifications which can increase workload, e.g. assessing for access arrangements; and
- a child, or children, whose needs require a great deal of support (in terms of time), e.g. those with very high levels of social, emotional and mental health SEMH difficulties.

This data is not drawn from, or comparable to, SENCO time allocations in the independent or special school sectors, given the different requirements and demands of each, and therefore should not be used as a guideline for time in these settings.

This data also does not include time required for other responsibilities that are not part of the SENCO role, e.g. teaching; planning, preparation and assessment (PPA) time; Designated Teacher of LAC; safeguarding; management of a Specialist Resource Provision; or non-SEN related SLT responsibilities.

Additionally, this data does not demonstrate the size or nature of the deployable support team around the SENCO, but assumes that there is one and that the size of the team is proportionate to the size and demographic of the school. A team might include a number of teaching assistants, administrative support, pastoral support workers etc. Further free guidance about maximising the impact of teaching assistant time can be found through the SEND Gateway, hosted by nasen.

Smaller than average size schools

The average primary school has 260 pupils (1.5 class entry); the average secondary school has 910 pupils (6 class entry).

Percentage of SEND (EHCP/SEN support): lower than average

For the purposes of this survey 'lower than average' is considered to be 6.7% or less.

School type (smaller than average size)	Recommended time allocation	Other advice and guidance to support decision making
Primary	1.5–2 days	Factors that would evidence a need for the higher, or even additional, time requirements would include:
Secondary	2.5–3 days	• 6 or more EHCPs. • Additional qualifications held by the SENCO, especially qualifications to assess (e.g. CCET, L7 SpLD). • A child in crisis requiring immediate and time-intensive support, e.g. significant SEMH.

Percentage of SEND (EHCP/SEN support): average

For the purposes of this survey 'average' is considered to be 11.7% (± 4%).

School type (smaller than average size)	Recommended time allocation	Other advice and guidance to support decision making
Primary	2–3 days	Factors that would evidence a need for the higher, or even additional, time requirements would include:
Secondary	3–4 days	• 6 or more EHCPs. • Additional qualifications held by the SENCO, especially qualifications to assess (e.g. CCET, L7 SpLD). • A child in crisis requiring immediate and time-intensive support, e.g. significant SEMH.

Percentage of SEND (EHCP/SEN support): higher than average

For the purposes of this survey 'higher than average' is considered to be 16.7% or more.

School type (smaller than average size)	Recommended time allocation	Other advice and guidance to support decision making
Primary	3–4 days	Factors that would evidence a need for the higher, or even additional, time requirements would include:
Secondary	4–5 days	• 6 or more EHCPs. • Additional qualifications held by the SENCO, especially qualifications to assess (e.g. CCET, L7 SpLD). • A child in crisis requiring immediate and time-intensive support, e.g. significant SEMH.

Average size schools

The average primary school has 260 pupils (1.5 class entry); the average secondary school has 910 pupils (6 class entry.)

Percentage of SEND (EHCP/SEN support): lower than average

For the purposes of this survey 'lower than average' is considered to be 6.7% or less.

School type (average size)	Recommended time allocation	Other advice and guidance to support decision making
Primary Secondary	2–3 days 3–4 days	Factors that would evidence a need for the higher, or even additional, time requirements would include: • 10 or more EHCPs. • Additional qualifications held by the SENCO, especially qualifications to assess (e.g. CCET, L7 SpLD). • A child in crisis requiring immediate and time-intensive support, e.g. significant SEMH.

Percentage of SEND (EHCP/SEN support): average

For the purposes of this survey 'average' is considered to be 11.7% (± 4%).

School type (average size)	Recommended time allocation	Other advice and guidance to support decision making
Primary Secondary	3–4 days 4–5 days	Factors that would evidence a need for the higher, or even additional, time requirements would include: • 10 or more EHCPs. • Additional qualifications held by the SENCO, especially qualifications to assess (e.g. CCET, L7 SpLD). • A child in crisis requiring immediate and time-intensive support, e.g. significant SEMH.

121

Percentage of SEND (EHCP/SEN support): higher than average

For the purposes of this survey 'higher than average' is considered to be 16.7% or more.

School type (average size)	Recommended time allocation	Other advice and guidance to support decision making
Primary	4–5 days	Factors that would evidence a need for the higher, or even additional, time requirements would include:
Secondary	5+ days*	
		• 10 or more EHCPs.
		• Additional qualifications held by the SENCO, especially qualifications to assess (e.g. CCET, L7 SpLD).
		• A child in crisis requiring immediate and time-intensive support, e.g. significant SEMH.

* A SENCO in this type of school may need another qualified SENCO to work an additional 1–2 days to support their workload. This may be in the form of an assistant SENCO or job share.

Larger than average size schools

The average primary school has 260 pupils (1.5 class entry); the average secondary school has 910 pupils (6 class entry.)

Percentage of SEND (EHCP/SEN support): lower than average

For the purposes of this survey 'lower than average' is considered to be 6.7% or less.

School type (larger than average size)	• Recommended time allocation	• Other advice and guidance to support decision making
Primary	3–4 days	Factors that would evidence a need for the higher, or even additional, time requirements would include:
Secondary	4–5 days	
		• 10 or more EHCPs.
		• Additional qualifications held by the SENCO, especially qualifications to assess (e.g. CCET, L7 SpLD).
		• A child in crisis requiring immediate and time-intensive support, e.g. significant SEMH.

Percentage of SEND (EHCP/SEN support): average

For the purposes of this survey 'average' is considered to be 11.7% (± 4%).

School type (Larger than average size)	Recommended Time Allocation	Other Advice & Guidance to support decision making
Primary	5+ days*	Factors which would evidence need of the higher, or even additional, time requirements would include: ● 16 or more EHCPs ● Additional qualifications held by the SENCO, especially qualifications to assess (e.g. CCET, L7 SpLD). ● A child in crisis requiring immediate and time-intensive support, e.g. significant SEMH.
Secondary	5+ days*	

* This data is predicted data based upon the number of SENCOs requesting 5 days, considering also the trend throughout the data from other settings which is reflected here. This data is predicted as there was not an option provided for more than 5 days (a limitation of the survey). Using this predicted time need, a SENCO in this type of school may need another qualified SENCO to work an additional 1–2 days to support their workload. This may be in the form of an assistant SENCO or job share.

Percentage of SEND (EHCP/SEN support): higher than average

For the purposes of this survey 'higher than average' is considered to be 16.7% or more.

School type (larger than average size)	Recommended time allocation	Other advice and guidance to support decision making
Primary	4–5 days	Factors that would evidence a need for the higher, or even additional, time requirements would include: ● 10 or more EHCPs (primary); 16 or more EHCPs (secondary). ● Additional qualifications held by the SENCO, especially qualifications to assess (e.g. CCET, L7 SpLD). ● A child in crisis requiring immediate and time-intensive support, e.g. significant SEMH.
Secondary	5+ days*	

* This data is predicted data based upon the number of SENCOs requesting 5 days, considering also the trend throughout the data from other settings which is reflected here. This data is predicted as there was not an option provided for more than 5 days (a limitation of the survey). Using this predicted time need, a SENCO in this type of school may need another qualified SENCO to work an additional 1–2 days to support their workload. This may be in the form of an assistant SENCO or job share.

123

References

Bowers, T., Dee, L. and West, M. (1998) 'The code in action: Some school perceptions of its user-friendliness', *Support for Learning*, 13 (3), pp. 99–104.

Children and Families Act 2014, ch. 6. Available at: www.legislation.gov.uk/ukpga/2014/6/pdfs/ukp ga_20140006_en.pdf (Accessed 1st August 2014).

Cole, B. A. (2005) 'Mission impossible? Special educational needs, inclusion and the re-conceptualisation of the role of the SENCo in England and Wales', *European Journal of Special Needs Education*, 20 (3), pp. 287–307.

Cowne, E. (2005) *The SENCO handbook: Working within a whole-school approach.* 5th edn. Abingdon, UK: David Fulton.

Curran, H., Moloney, H., Heavey, A. and Boddison, A. (2018) *It's about time: The impact of SENCO workload on the professional and the school.* Available at: www.bathspa.ac.uk/schools/ education/research/senco-workload/ (Accessed 3rd January 2019).

Department for Education (DfE). (1994) *The Code of Practice on the identification and assessment of special educational needs.* London: HMSO.

Department for Education (DfE) and Department of Health (DoH). (2015) *Special educational needs and disability Code of Practice: 0–25 years.* Available at: www.gov.uk/government/uploads/ system/uploads/attachment_data/file/398815/SEND_Code_of_Practice_January_2015.pdf (Accessed 1st February 2015).

Department for Education and Skills (DfES). (2001) *Special educational needs Code of Practice.* Available at: webarchive.nationalarchives.gov.uk/20130401151715/www.education.gov.uk/publi cations/eOrderingDownload/0581-2001-SEN-CodeofPractice.pdf (Accessed 20th September 2014).

Derrington, C. (1997) 'A case for unpacking? Redefining the role of the SENCO in the light of the Code of Practice', *Support for Learning*, 12 (3), pp. 111–115.

Garner, P. (1996) '"Go forth and coordinate!" What special needs coordinators think about the code of practice', *School Organisation*, 16 (2), pp. 179–186.

Hallett, F. and Hallett, G. (eds.) (2010) *Transforming the role of the SENCo: Achieving the National Award for SEN coordination.* Maidenhead, UK: Oxford University Press.

Kearns, H. (2005) 'Exploring the experiential learning of special educational needs coordinators', *Journal of In-Service Education*, 31 (1), pp. 131–150.

Layton, L. (2005) 'Special educational needs coordinators and leadership: A role too far?', *Support for Learning*, 20 (2), pp. 53–59.

Lingard, T. (2001) 'Does the Code of Practice help secondary school SENCos to improve learning?', *British Journal of Special Education*, 28 (4), pp. 187–190.

Mackenzie, S. (2007) 'A review of recent developments in the role of the SENCo in the UK', *British Journal of Special Education*, 34 (4), pp. 212–218.

National College of Teaching and Learning. (2014) *National Award for special educational needs co-ordination: Learning outcomes.* Available at: www.gov.uk/government/uploads/system/uploads/ attachment_data/file/354172/nasc-learning-outcomes-final.pdf (Accessed 1st September 2014).

Pearson, S. (2008) 'Deafened by silence or by the sound of footsteps? An investigation of the recruitment, induction and retention of special educational needs coordinators (SENCOs) in England', *Journal of Research in Special Educational Needs*, 8 (2), pp. 96–110.

Pearson, S., Mitchell, R. and Rapti, M. (2015) 'I will be "fighting" even more for pupils with SEN: SENCOs' role predictions in the changing English policy context', *Journal of Research in Special Educational Needs*, 15 (1), pp. 48–56.

Pearson, S. and Ralph, S. (2007) 'The identity of SENCos: Insights through images', *Journal of Research in Special Educational Needs*, 7 (1), pp. 36–45.

Qureshi, S. (2014) 'Herding cats or getting heard: The SENCo-teacher dynamic and its impact on teachers' classroom practice', *Support for Learning*, 29 (3), pp. 217–229.

Rosen-Webb, S. (2011) 'Nobody tells you how to be a SENCo', *British Journal of Special Education*, 38 (4), pp. 159–168.

Szwed, C. (2007a) 'Remodelling policy and practice: The challenge for staff working with children with special educational needs', *Educational Review*, 59 (2), pp. 147–160.

Szwed, C. (2007b) 'Managing from the middle? Tensions and dilemmas in the role of the primary school special educational needs coordinator', *School Leadership & Management*, 27 (5), pp. 437–451.

Szwed, C. (2007c) 'Reconsidering the role of the primary special educational needs co-ordinator: Policy, practice and future priorities', *British Journal of Special Education*, 34 (2), pp. 96–104.

The Education (Special Educational Needs Co-ordinators) (England) (Amendment) Regulations 2009 (SI 2009/1387). Available at: http://dera.ioe.ac.uk/10702/5/uksi_20091387_en.pdf (Accessed 14th September 2013).

The future SENCO role

This book concludes by considering your SENCO role going forwards and the way in which it may change in the future. Nationally, the educational landscape is changing rapidly, and this will impact on how your role develops over time. Therefore, this chapter will explore some of the key changes which have recently occurred within wider educational policy, including the advancement of the multi-academies trust agenda, as well as changes to accessing services, and how this may impact on your role.

However, the chapter will also consider how you wish to shape your future SENCO role. The book, so far, has explored ways in which you can shape your SENCO role predominantly at the start of your career. Yet, the potential for growth within the SENCO role is significant, therefore the book will conclude with a series of prompts to help you to consider how you can develop your SENCO career in the longer term.

In summary, this chapter will focus on:

- wider educational changes and how these may impact on the future SENCO role; and
- shaping your future SENCO role.

Wider educational changes and how these may impact on the future SENCO role

The role of the SENCO, and the development of inclusive education, cannot be viewed in isolation. As Norwich states, the SEN system is 'interdependent' of the wider education system (2014, p. 404), which infers that broader changes to our educational system are likely to impact on the role of the SENCO.

Multi-academy trusts

It could be argued that one of the most significant changes is the increased focus on, and the development of, the academies agenda, specifically the development of groups of academies typically known as multi-academy trusts (MATs). It was the introduction of the 2010 Academies Act that promoted growth in this area, with the government stating that it 'hopes and expects' that all schools will convert to academy status (DfE,

2016, p. 8). Keddie (2016) suggests that the policy goals of academisation include increasing parental choice, which it could be argued complements the principles of parental involvement and engagement in the SEND Code of Practice (DfE and DoH, 2015). However, it could be reasoned that a change in school structures is likely to impact on the execution of the SENCO role.

Legislation in relation to the role of the SENCO does not yet take into account the introduction of MATs. The SEND Code of Practice (DfE and DoH, 2015) refers to the mandatory nature of the role in standalone academies, and does not mention how the role could be executed under a multi-academy trust model, while Department for Education guidance (2016) suggests that one SENCO could work across a number of schools in a MAT. The NASUWT (2016), however, suggests that where MATs exist over several local authorities, there is the potential for conflict when SENCOs are trying to negotiate local policies as well as MAT policies.

The move towards MATs provides a change to the school leadership structure, which may impact on the strategic nature of the SENCO role in the future, and further indicates the importance of either the SENCO being part of the senior leadership team (SLT), or having a strong advocate for the SENCO on the SLT. The MAT agenda may provide an opportunity for the introduction of new leadership models (Hill, 2016), which could, in turn, provide an opportunity for a reconceptualisation of the SENCO position in relation to the SLT. If management structures within the school, and wider MAT, are changing, this is a chance for the SENCO to raise the issue of seniority and/or status of the position, or to reconsider how they see their role developing within the MAT. For example, a development opportunity for a SENCO may be the Head of Inclusion across the MAT. It is, therefore, important to consider your SENCO role if you are part of a MAT, and to explore this with senior colleagues.

Certainly, one positive aspect of developments in this area is the potential growth of support networks. SENCOs may be able to access school-to-school support, as well as share good practices and resources via a MAT (DfE, 2016). As a result, this may increase the capacity of the SENCO within their own school due to their access to additional support and resources. This may also alleviate some of the issues reported by SENCOs related to isolation. However, this is likely to be dependent on availability and expertise within the MAT and, in particular, capacity (Riddell, 2016). It may be that support is facilitated for you, or you may find that you need to take the initiative to bring together the group to create a network.

The increased focus on advocacy

In addition to the advancement of multi-academy trusts, there has been a raft of changes which have taken place nationally in the world of education. It could be argued that these directly impact on the SENCO role, particularly in terms of being an advocate. For example, there have been a number of changes, especially related to curriculum and assessment, and including the introduction of the new curriculum (DfE, 2014), which brings with it a different set of challenges for the SENCO. It would be impossible to cite all the changes occurring, particularly as these are ongoing. However, Glazzard (2014) suggests that the advancement of inclusive policy is already problematic, in part due to the tension between the inclusion agenda and the standards agenda (Ellis and Tod, 2014; Norwich, 2014). Given the changes that are occurring, we could hypothesise that this advancement may be further hindered. School leaders, for example the governing body and the head teacher, have a central role to play in developing inclusive policy in their schools. However, without an advocate for SEN and inclusive policy from within the school, for example the SENCO, there is a 'potential loss of a strong voice for inclusive strategic school-wide practice' (Tissot, 2013, p. 34). As such, this suggests that as wider, educational changes are enacted, the voice of the SENCO advocating for specific groups, and the potential impact of policy on them, may need to be even stronger. This is especially true if some of the aforementioned changes may be perceived as having a negative impact on vulnerable groups, particularly learners with special educational needs.

It could be further argued that the need for an advocacy role, at a strategic level, for inclusive principles and provision for children with SEN is particularly important when the changes are set against a backdrop of wider education budget cuts (National Audit Office, 2016). Schools are not currently accountable for their SEN spending, akin to the pupil premium processes. In addition to this, 'there are anecdotal reports of some academy schools being reluctant to accept students with statements' (Norwich and Black, 2015, p. 131; Trafford, 2016), which may be due to the link between the outputs of the school, for example exam results, and the inputs, the children who are on roll (Rayner, 2017), or due to concerns related to the lack of funding required to meet a pupil's needs (Cassidy and Garner, 2016; Goddard, 2016). Whilst this may not be your experience as a SENCO, it is imperative to consider how such factors may impact on your school, and your role, in the future.

Finally, the introduction of the SEND Code of Practice (DfE and DoH, 2015) has signified a different way of working with parents; historically, SENCOs have communicated with parents, and now the SEND Code of Practice states that SENCOs need to collaborate and proactively engage with parents in decision making. It could be argued that this may provide SENCOs with a challenge, as the relationship has changed; there is a need to foster these *new style* relationships. In addition to this, the SENCO may find that they need to advocate for this new style relationship across all areas of the school to ensure that the principles of the SEND Code of Practice are met in their setting. This also implies that additional time will need to be allocated to the SENCO role to facilitate such relationships.

The increased focus on supporting colleagues

In addition to advocating across the school for parents, the SENCO may find that they need to support colleagues with how to develop effective working relationships, which move beyond engagement and towards collaboration. SENCOs may find that they need to plan for specific support for varying groups of staff, regarding how they work with and engage with parents as equal partners.

However, it is likely that training needs will extend beyond the additional support needed for parental engagement. Since the introduction of the SEND Code of Practice (DfE and DoH, 2015), there has been an overall reduction in the number of children identified as having additional needs in school. In 2010, a reported 18.3% of children had SEN (DfE, 2015); from 2014 to 2015 there was then a marked drop from 17.9% to 15.4% (DfE, 2015), based on the January 2015 census data. In January 2018, the number of pupils with SEN was 14.6% (DfE, 2018). Research (Curran et al., 2017) has illustrated that there has been a myriad of reasons for the reduction in numbers, including a review of the definition of SEN and its application in schools, removal of the 'school action' band, and a greater focus on more complex children in school. In the shorter term, this raises questions as to how the reduction of registers and the removal of children has been communicated and justified to parents and teachers. In the longer term, however, such a change also has implications for class and subject teachers, whose classes may contain an increasingly diverse range of learners whose needs have not changed or disappeared. Whilst Szwed (2007) has previously suggested that teachers will need to be increasingly concerned with the needs of all learners, in response to inclusion, the national statistics, alongside current research (Curran et al., 2017) suggest that it is the classification which has changed, rather than the student populations. Whilst this will have implications for initial teacher training (ITT), from the perspective of the SENCO, there are implications for CPD in their school. SENCOs may find that they need to offer specific support and training regarding SEN and inclusive practice, to new and experienced teachers, to ensure that the requirements of the national curriculum (DfE, 2014) and the SEND Code of Practice (DfE and DoH, 2015) – to respond to the needs of all learners – are being met.

Something to think about

Consider the longer-term development plan for your school, as well as anticipated changes happening in the wider world of educational policy.

Which of these are likely to impact on either your role, or on children with additional needs in your school? How will this impact on both the facilitation and focus of your role?

Shaping your future SENCO role

Whilst there are a number of external factors which are likely to impact on the facilitation of your role, it is important to consider how you see, not only SEN and inclusive practice developing in your school, but how you see yourself, professionally developing as a SENCO. There are a number of ways in which you can begin to develop your role, both within and outside of your school.

Things to consider:

- Keep learning. A key part of the SENCO role is to keep abreast of developments in your area. Having completed the NA SENCO, you may decide that you want to carry on with formal learning and use your 60 credits at Masters level towards a full Masters degree. Your local university will be able to support you with this. However, learning does not have to be formal. Look at the various courses offered locally or remotely. This may include webinars from nasen or the British Dyslexia Association. Pick up an article and read about a different area of SEN. Visiting other SENCOs in different settings can also be an excellent way to develop and enhance your role.
- Becoming a mentor on the NA SENCO. Every NA SENCO is set up differently, however there may be an opportunity for you to work with your local provider, supporting new SENCOs.
- Creating your own cluster. If you do not currently access a SENCO cluster, consider how you can create one of your own. Think about how you will structure this. Teach meets can be a great way to get groups of SENCOs together to share good practice.
- Working alongside the local authority. There may be opportunities for you to work alongside your local authority colleagues, for example, taking part in needs assessment panels.
- Explore engagement opportunity with groups such as Research SEND, Whole School SEND or nasen. There is a drive towards sharing good practices, as well as linking theory and practice. Consider getting involved, either through attending, going to a working group or presenting!

In summary

The SENCO has a critical role to play within schools, for children, parents and colleagues, regarding provision and advocacy for children with additional needs, as well as in determining and influencing wider policy priorities. Throughout the facilitation of the role, the SENCO will need to think about the various activities they undertake to fulfil their role, both operationally and strategically. In addition to this, the SENCO role is not static and is one which is susceptible to change in relation to wider educational reform, but also offers the individual scope for professional development. Such change can bring uncertainty to those in the role but, equally, this can make for an exciting role full of possibilities for not only the SENCO themselves, but also all those they work with. As such, the importance of this crucial role in schools can be argued now more than ever.

References

Academies Act 2010, ch. 32. Available at: www.legislation.gov.uk/ukpga/2010/32/pdfs/ukpga_20100032_en.pdf (Accessed 30th June 2017).

Cassidy, S. and Garner, R. (2016) *Academies turn away children with special needs to 'cherry-pick' pupils, charity warns*. Available at: www.independent.co.uk/news/education/education-news/academies-turn-away-children-with-special-needs-to-cherry-pick-pupils-charity-warns-a6795001.html (Accessed 10th January 2016).

Curran, H., Mortimore, T. and Riddell, R. (2017) 'Special educational needs and disabilities reforms 2014: SENCos' perspectives of the first six months.' *British Journal of Special Education*, 44 (1), pp. 46–64.

Department for Education (DfE). (2014) *National curriculum in England: Framework for key stages 1 to 4*. Available at: www.gov.uk/government/publications/national-curriculum-in-england-framework-for-key-stages-1-to-4/the-national-curriculum-in-england-framework-for-key-stages-1-to-4 (Accessed 4th September 2014).

Department for Education (DfE). (2015) *Special educational needs in England: January 2015*. Available at: www.gov.uk/government/statistics/special-educational-needs-in-england-january-2015 (Accessed 24th October 2015).

Department for Education (DfE). (2016) *Multi-academy trusts: Good practice for guidance and expectations for growth*. Available at: www.gov.uk/government/uploads/system/uploads/attachment_data/file/576240/Multi-academy_trusts_good_practice_guidance_and_expectations_for_growth.pdf (Accessed 3rd July 2017).

Department for Education (DfE). (2018) *Special educational needs in England: January 2018*. Available at: https://assets.publishing.service.gov.uk/government/uploads/system/uploads/attachment_data/file/729208/SEN_2018_Text.pdf (Accessed 20th January 2019).

Department for Education (DfE) and Department of Health (DoH). (2015) *Special educational needs and disability code of practice: 0–25 years*. Available at: www.gov.uk/government/uploads/system/

uploads/attachment_data/file/398815/SEND_Code_of_Practice_January_2015.pdf (Accessed 1st February 2015).

Ellis, S. and Tod, J. (2014) 'Chapter 5. Special educational needs and inclusion: Reflection, renewal and reality.' *Journal of Research in Special Educational Needs*, 14 (3), pp. 205–210.

Glazzard, J. (2014) 'The standards agenda: Reflections of a special educational needs co-ordinator.' *Support for Learning*, 29 (1), pp. 39–53.

Goddard, V. (2016) '*Academies guilty of the most blatant gaming of all: A school place only for the brightest*'. 29th March 2016. Available at: www.theguardian.com/education/2016/mar/29/academy-school-place-educating-essex-special-needs (Accessed 12th July 2016).

Hill, R. (2016) 'Where is the MAT agenda going?' *Robert Hill Education Blog*. 31st October 2016. Available at: https://roberthilleducationblog.com/ (Accessed 3rd November 2016).

Keddie, A. (2016) 'Academisation, school collaboration and the primary school sector in England: A story of six school leaders.' *School Leadership & Management*, 36 (2), pp. 169–183.

NASUWT. (2016) *Briefing for SENCos on the special educational need and disability (SEND) reforms*. Available at: www.nasuwt.org.uk/uploads/assets/uploaded/3acc95d7-53e3-4706-a2dd8163bc937f97.pdf (Accessed 3rd July 2017).

National Audit Office. (2016) *Financial sustainability of schools*. Available at: www.nao.org.uk/report/financial-sustainability-in-schools/ (Accessed 4th January 2017).

Norwich, B. (2014) 'Changing policy and legislation and its effects on inclusive and special education: A perspective from England.' *British Journal of Special Education*, 41 (4), p. 40.

Norwich, B. and Black, A. (2015) 'The placement of secondary school students with Statements of special educational needs in the more diversified system of English secondary schooling.' *British Journal Of Special Education*, 42 (2), pp. 128–151.

Rayner, S. (2017) 'Admissions policies and risks to equity and educational inclusion in the context of school reform in England.' *Management in Education*, 31 (1), pp. 27–32.

Riddell, R. (2016) *Equity, Trust and the Self-Improving Schools System*. Stoke-on-Trent, UK: Trentham Books.

Szwed, C. (2007) 'Reconsidering the role of the primary special educational needs co-ordinator: Policy, practice and future priorities.' *British Journal of Special Education*, 34 (2), pp. 96–104.

Tissot, C. (2013) 'The role of SENCos as leaders.' *British Journal of Special Education*, 40 (1), pp. 33–40.

Trafford, B. (2016) *Funding cuts and the acceleration of academisation mean special needs will continue to suffer*. Available at: www.tes.com/ (Accessed on 8th August 2016).

Appendix
Acronyms

DfE	Department of Education
DfEE	Department for Education and Employment
DfES	Department for Education and Skills
DoH	Department of Health
EHC plan	Education, Health and Care plan
IEP	Individual Education Plan
HEI	Higher Education Institute
HMSO	Her Majesty's Stationery Office
ITT	Initial teacher training
LA	Local authority
LEA	Local Education Authority
LSA	Learning Support Assistant
MoE	Ministry of Education
NAO	National Audit Office
NASEN	National Association of Special Educational Needs
NA SENCO	The National Award for Special Educational Needs Coordination
Ofsted	The Office for Standards in Education
QFT	Quality First Teaching
SEMH	Social, emotional and mental health
SEN	Special Educational Needs
SENCO	Special Educational Needs Coordinator
SEND	Special Educational Needs and Disability
SENDA	Special Educational Needs and Disability Act
SLT	Senior leadership team
TA	Teaching assistant
TDA	The Training and Development Agency for Schools
UNCRC	United Nations Convention on the Rights of the Child

Index

advocates: growing your team of 52–53; for inclusion 32–33, 51–52, 72–73, 126; for parents 32, 79, 95–97; for pupils 32–33, 36; for the SENCO 19; for staff 129

audit: family experiences 90–91; pupil experiences 88; skills of staff 16, 64, 66–67, 69, 74–75

Children and Families Act (2014) 1, 6, 13, 49, 78; EHC needs assessment 107; role of SENCO 23, 52

Code of Practice on the identification and assessment of SEN (1994) 2, 8–9, 111

communication 51, 54; with parents and pupils 81, 96; with staff 69, 75

continuing professional development 36–38, 60, 67–68, 74–75, 89, 117

cultural change 23, 25, 47

data: as a strategic tool 25; use of 16, 66–67

development plan 45, 63, 73, 92, 129; as a strategic tool 54–55

disability: inclusive model 30–32; medical model 29; tensions with models 31–32

DISS report 61

Education, Health and Care (EHC) plans 2, 54, 64, 98, 105–108

educational policy 33, 72, 127–128; in relation to SEN policy 72

ethos 27–29, 32–33, 54, 79, 87

governing body 11, 50, 53, 128; role of SENCO 6, 10–11, 22, 42, 56, 103–104

graduated approach 13; parent and pupil involvement 85–86; SENCO role 13, 16, 62; teacher role 62

House of Commons Select Committee Report (2006) 1, 9, 22, 41

inclusion: advocating for 32–33, 51; agenda 128; definition 29; development of 28; ethos 23, 27–28, 43; SENCO responsibility 9, 24, 60; tensions 30, 31, 36, 72, 128; whole school approaches 43–46, 54–55

Initial Teacher Training 68, 129

INSET 65, 68

key worker system 89, 94–95, 99, 113

Lamb Inquiry 1, 83

local authority 9, 107–108

Local Offer 1–2, 94, 110

Multi Academy Trust 42, 53, 68, 70, 113, 115, 126–127

National Award for SEN Coordination (NA SENCO) 2, 12, 26, 48, 130; introduction of 11–12; management of 50, 52, 112, 114–117

National Curriculum 2, 28–30, 66

networks: parents 94; SENCO 55, 68, 73, 111, 113–115, 127

newly qualified teachers 74–75

outside agencies 16, 70, 92–93, 97, 106–107

parents: EHC plans 98; importance of relationships 83–87, 129; individual approaches 95–98; multi-agency meetings 97–98; participation 1–2, 11, 50; policy context 78–82; potential barriers 84–87; whole school approaches 51, 55, 90–95; working with 13, 16, 49–51, 55, 71, 73, 128

provision mapping 25, 110

pupils: diagnosis 31–32; importance of relationships 82–83; inclusion of 28–29; individual approaches 89–90; potential barriers 86–87; provision 10–11, 16; whole school approaches 10, 55, 62, 88–89

qualified teacher status 23, 47

referral process, in-house 16, 71–72, 108–109

SEN Code of Practice (2001) 2; definition of SEN 34; introduction of 8–9, 24, 102; SENCO role 12, 14, 41
SEN definition 28, 34; tensions with 35–36
SEN governor 112; advocating 45, 50; understanding the SENCO role 103–104, 117; working with 15, 17, 19, 53, 55
SEN information report 2; parents 92–93; SENCO activities 13, 15, 17, 63, 70, 84
SEN policy: parents 92–93; SENCO role 13, 15, 17, 24, 58; teachers 74
SEN support 82, 84–86
SENCO regulations 9–12, 23, 41, 45, 47–48, 115
SENCO responsibilities 12–13
SENCO role: current 12–14; future 126–130; historical development 6–12; informing colleagues 103–104; as a leader 23–27, 59, 63; in practice 14–17, 111–112; shaping 17–19
SEND Code of Practice (2015) 1; families 83–86; graduated approach 62; guidance 6, 34; inclusion 29, 31; needs assessment 107–108; principles 2, 78–82, 128; pupils 82, 85–86, 88–89; SENCO role 12–14, 22, 41, 52, 59, 102; teachers' role 33, 46, 58, 61–62, 68; working with parents 128
SEND reforms 1, 2, 49, 64, 78, 81, 110
senior leadership team 14, 22–27, 41–44; advantages and disadvantages 44; lack of membership 45–46; liaison with 51–52, 65; status 45–46
status 6, 22, 43, 44–49; developing 49, 51–55
strategic leadership 6, 22–27, 30–38, 42–44, 51–56; inclusive practice 63; managing the role 102, 108, 111, 127–128; SENCO role 9, 14; setting priorities 37, 50, 55, 96; tensions 48; working with parents 91–92
support staff 48, 61, 75, 94; SENCO regulations 11; working with 14, 16, 46, 113

teachers: audit 64–66; communicating with 54–55; new to school 74; role and responsibility 32–33, 46, 58, 61–63; supporting 11, 14, 59–60, 67–73, 89, 129

United Nations Convention on the Rights of the Child (UNCRC) (1989) 82

Warnock report 7–9, 28–29, 34, 83
workload: managing 103–109, 118–123; National Award for SEN Coordination 114–118; SENCO 8, 50, 94, 102–103; teachers 61

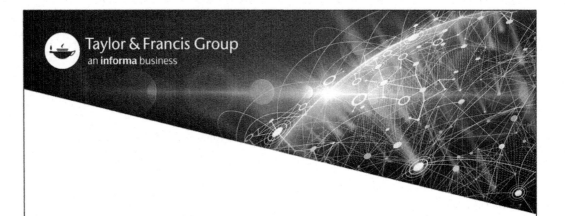